Resounding praise for

Emotional Inheritance

A THERAPIST, HER PATIENTS, AND THE LEGACY OF TRAUMA

by Galit Atlas, PhD

"Beautiful, artistic, and elegant. Dr. Atlas skillfully uses stories from her practice to explore the archeology of transgenerational trauma. The descriptions of the therapeutic process pull you in; you come to know both patient and therapist. In doing so, you cannot help but reflect on your own journey. *Emotional Inheritance* is a gem for anyone, but it is an essential read for those seeking to understand trauma, therapy, and the healing process."

— Bruce D. Perry, MD, PhD, coauthor
(with Oprah Winfrey) of *What Happened to You?*

"A powerful, lucid, deeply empathic exploration of the legacy of generational trauma, *Emotional Inheritance* makes clear that Galit Atlas is not only a gifted psychoanalyst, but a gifted writer as well. I loved this book and was stirred by it."

— Dani Shapiro, author of *Inheritance*

"An illuminating book. The stories Dr. Atlas shares reveal the potency of our inherited wounds, showing how the experiences of our ancestors shape our lives in quiet but far-reaching ways, and how we all have the potential to heal."

— Lori Gottlieb, author of *Maybe You Should Talk to Someone*

"Dr. Atlas writes with profound living compassion for those who have carried, in their bodies, minds, hearts, spirits, and souls, the most often unspoken and secret traumas of their own hurt elders. As a first-generation American child growing up in my tough family of war refugees, deportees—the ethnically cleansed, struggling immigrants—I humbly assert that I know about generational traumas in depth. I recognize Dr. Atlas as one who writes in full, knowing detail about what I call in my work 'the generational wound.'"

— Dr. Clarissa Pinkola Estés Reyés, author of
Women Who Run with the Wolves

"With elegance, Galit Atlas explains the troubling and nourishing aspects of our emotional inheritances. She deftly shows why the hurts and stuckness that can plague us can be faced and, yes, dissolved. Contemporary psychoanalysis at its best. And good storytelling too."

— Susie Orbach, author of *Fat Is a Feminist Issue*

"An intimate, textured, and compassionate exploration of intergenerational trauma, how it is carried and transmitted within families, and how it can be skillfully invited in, recognized, attenuated, and perhaps resolved through the therapeutic relationship, metabolizing what has hitherto not been named or nameable."

— Jon Kabat-Zinn, author of *The Healing Power of Mindfulness*

"This book is full of great wisdom, expertise, and humanity. An important, terrific, gripping read."

— Dr. Anne Alvarez, author of *Live Company*

"*Emotional Inheritance* offers extraordinary insight to readers who feel stuck in lifelong patterns and sense they are haunted by ghosts from their family's past. Dr. Atlas deftly shares her own history and those of her patients while seamlessly weaving in the relevant psychological research. Dr. Atlas's book reads like a propulsive page-turner while also offering deep psychological insights about inherited trauma and family secrets. This book will undoubtedly change lives and help readers unlock their unfulfilled potential."

 — Christie Tate, author of *Group*

"Galit Atlas has given us a gift with her book *Emotional Inheritance*. With warmth and compassion, she is able to show the reader the ways our present challenges could be linked to our inherited past. Using patient stories and her own experiences, we are taken on a journey of discovery. By sharing these stories, she gives us a glimpse behind our own curtains and helps us understand that if we are open to the possibility of hope, now might be the right time to break the silence our ancestors have held for so long."

 — Sharon Salzberg, author of *Real Happiness*

"Galit Atlas's *Emotional Inheritance* is insightful, perceptive, and provocative—but also tender, touching, and personal. Talented clinicians are not always talented writers, but Dr. Atlas is, and her stories will stay with you. The world of epigenetics is in its infancy for most of us, but Dr. Atlas uses ordinary language to explain how we are born with psychological legacies that we cannot escape but which we can, with her help, understand."

 — Juliet Rosenfeld, author of *The State of Disbelief*

"Galit Atlas takes up Tolstoy's assertion — 'Happy families are all alike; every unhappy family is unhappy in its own way' — as she narrates the ways in which traumas are uniquely held within families. Atlas tells the layered stories of her patients as their traumas reverberate with her own history of trauma and loss. The intimacy of the storytelling captures the recognition and repair that Atlas undertakes with her patients. Together they exhume the secrets and the ghosts that carry and bury trauma, pulling the reader into the present through the past in order to break into the potential that is the future. Such potential is not a simple, sunny vale. Unhappy families are not made unthinkingly happy. But as Atlas demonstrates through her graceful generosity, bringing secrets and ghosts into the daylight offers the potential for new stories, more life, and the liberation called happiness."

— Ken Corbett, PhD, author of *A Murder Over a Girl*

"A truly wise and daring book, *Emotional Inheritance* is an utterly compelling account of how the unconscious passage of trauma from one generation to the next is revealed in psychotherapy. With her special gift for evocative narrative, Dr. Atlas makes us present as witnesses to powerful stories of sorrows held in secret, of children who carry those sorrows forward, knowing without knowing what darkens their lives. Illuminating the meaning of such histories with splendid insights, this book will deeply satisfy whoever has wondered what psychoanalysis can offer in the present world."

— Dr. Jessica Benjamin, author of *The Bonds of Love*

Emotional Inheritance

ALSO BY GALIT ATLAS

The Enigma of Desire:
Sex, Longing, and Belonging in Psychoanalysis

Dramatic Dialogue: Contemporary Clinical Practice

When Minds Meet: The Work of Lewis Aron (edited)

Emotional Inheritance

A THERAPIST, HER PATIENTS, AND THE LEGACY OF TRAUMA

Galit Atlas, PhD

Little, Brown Spark
New York Boston London

*This book is dedicated
to the memory of Lewis Aron.*

In those days people will no longer say,
"The parents have eaten sour grapes,
and the children's teeth are set on edge."

— JEREMIAH 31:29

Contents

CONTENTS

Emotional Inheritance

A Trace in the Mind

EVERY FAMILY CARRIES some history of trauma. Every trauma is held within a family in a unique way and leaves its emotional mark on those who are yet to be born.

In the last decade, contemporary psychoanalysis and empirical research have expanded the literature on epigenetics and inherited trauma, investigating the ways in which trauma is transmitted from one generation to the next and held in our minds and bodies as our own. In studying the intergenerational transmission of trauma, clinicians investigate how our ancestors' trauma is passed down as an emotional inheritance, leaving a trace in our minds and in those of future generations.

Emotional Inheritance is about silenced experiences that belong not only to us but to our parents, grandparents, and great-grandparents, and about the ways they impact our lives. It is these secrets that often keep us from living to our full potential. They affect our mental and physical health, create gaps between what we want for ourselves and what we are able to have, and haunt us like ghosts. This book will introduce the ties connecting past, present, and future and ask: how do we move forward?

From a very young age, my siblings and I learned to recognize what wasn't acceptable to talk about. We never asked about death. We tried not to mention sex, and it was better not to be too sad, too angry or disappointed, and absolutely not too loud. My parents didn't burden us with unhappiness, and they believed in optimism. When they described their childhoods, they were painted in beautiful colors, hiding trauma, poverty, and the pain of racism and immigration.

Both my parents were young children when their families left everything behind and emigrated to Israel, my father from Iran and my mother from Syria. Both grew up with six siblings in poor neighborhoods and struggled not only with poverty but also with the prejudice that came with being from an ethnic group considered inferior in Israel in the 1950s.

I knew that my father had two sisters who got sick and died when they were toddlers, before he was born, and that as a baby he was very ill himself and almost didn't survive. His father, my grandfather, who was blind from birth, needed my father to go to work with him, to sell newspapers on the street. As a child I was aware that my father hadn't gone to school and had worked to support his family since he was seven years old. He taught me how to work hard, as he longed for me to get an education that he could never afford for himself.

Like my father, my mother had also struggled as a baby with life-threatening illness. She had lost her oldest brother when she was ten years old, an enormous trauma for the whole family. My mother didn't have many childhood memories and therefore those are unknown to me. I'm not sure my parents ever realized how similar their histories were, how their bond was silently tied with illness, poverty, early loss, and shame.

Like many other families, our family colluded and shared the unspoken understanding that silence was the best way to erase what was unpleasant. The assumption in those days was that what you don't remember won't hurt you. But what if what you don't remember is in fact remembered, in spite of your best efforts?

I was their first child, and their traumatic past lived in my body.

There were wars where I grew up, and so often we, the kids, felt frightened, not fully aware that we were being raised in the shadow of the Holocaust, and that violence, loss, and endless grief were our national heritage.

The Yom Kippur War, by then the fifth war since 1948, broke out when I was only two years old. My sister was born on the first day of that war. Like all the other men, my father was called to serve in the army. I was left with a neighbor while my mother went alone to the hospital to give birth to my sister. The massive attack on Israel took everyone by surprise, and many wounded soldiers were rushed into the hospitals, which then became too crowded for women in labor. The women were moved to the hallways.

I don't remember a lot from that war, but as it usually is with childhood experiences, it was all perceived as pretty normal. For years to come, the school had a monthly "war drill." We children practiced walking quietly into the shelters, happy that instead of studying we were playing board games in the shelter and joking about the missile that might hit or the terrorists who would come with weapons and take us hostage. We were taught that nothing should be too difficult to handle, that danger was a normal part of life, and that all we needed was to be brave and keep a sense of humor.

I was never afraid at school; only at night did I worry that a terrorist might choose our house from all the other houses in the country, and then I wouldn't be able to save my family. I thought about all the good places people used to hide during the Holocaust: the basement, the attic, behind the library, in the closet. The secret was to make sure to always keep quiet.

But I wasn't so good at being quiet. As a teenager, I started making music, wondering if all I needed was to make noise and be heard. When I stood on stages, music was the magic. It gave voice to what I could not otherwise speak out loud. It was my protest against the unspoken.

Then, in 1982, the Lebanon War erupted and I was old enough to recognize that something terrible was happening. To the school's memorial wall were added more and more names, this time of young people we knew. Parents who had lost their boys came to the school for the ceremony of Memorial Day. I was proud to be the one singing for them, looking straight into their eyes and making sure I didn't cry because then I would ruin the song and someone else might have to take my place behind the mic. We ended the ceremony every year with "Shir La Shalom" ("A Song for Peace"), one of the most well-known Israeli songs. We sang for peace from the depth of our hearts. We wanted to have a new beginning and liberate our future.

I grew up on our parents' promise that by the time the children were eighteen and had to serve in the army, there would be no more wars. But that, to this day, has not happened. I served in the army as a musician, praying for peace, traveling from one army base to another, crossing borders, singing for the soldiers. I was a nineteen-year-old soldier when the Gulf War started.

We were on the road and the rock-and-roll music we played was loud, so loud that we had to make sure we didn't miss the sound of the sirens and could run to the shelters to put on our gas masks in time. At some point, we decided to give up on the masks and the shelters and instead ran to the roofs every time there was a siren so we could watch the missiles from Iraq and try to guess where they would fall. After each thunderous explosion, we would go back to our music and play it even louder.

We sang for the soldiers, who were also our childhood friends, neighbors, and siblings. And when they teared up, as they often did, I felt the power of touching another heart with my own, voicing the unspeakable. Our music expressed so much of what no one could say out loud: that we were scared but were not allowed to admit it even to ourselves, that we were still too young and wanted to go home, fall in love, travel far away. That we wanted normal lives but we were not sure what "normal" meant. Making music and singing out loud were meaningful and liberating. It was the beginning of my journey of a search for truths, the unveiling of the emotional inheritance within me.

Eventually, some years later, I left my homeland, moved to New York City, and began studying the unspeakable — all those silent memories, feelings, and desires that are outside awareness. I became a psychoanalyst, exploring the unconscious.

A TRACE IN THE MIND

The analysis of the mind, like a mystery story, is an investigation. We know that Sigmund Freud, the great sleuth of the unconscious mind, was a big fan of Sherlock Holmes and maintained a large library of detective fiction. In some ways, Freud borrowed Holmes's method: gathering evidence, searching for a truth beneath the surface truth, seeking out hidden realities.

Like detectives, my patients and I try to follow the signs and listen not only to what they say but also to their pauses, to the music of that which is unknown to both of us. It is delicate work, collecting reminiscences of childhood, of what was said or done, listening to the omissions, to stories untold. Looking for clues, piecing these together into a picture, we ask, What really happened and to whom?

The secrets of the mind include not only our own life experiences but also those that we unknowingly carry with us: the memories, feelings, and traumas that we inherit from previous generations.

It was after World War II when psychoanalysts first began examining the impact of trauma on the next generation. Many of those analysts were Jews who had escaped Europe. Their patients were Holocaust survivors and later the offspring of those trauma survivors, children who carried some unconscious trace of their ancestors' pain.

Starting in the 1970s, neuroscience validated the psychoanalytic findings that survivors' trauma — even the darkest secrets they never talked about — had a real effect on their children's and grandchildren's lives. In the 1990s, studies were focused on epigenetics, the nongenetic influences and modifications of gene expression. They analyzed how genes were altered in the descendants of trauma survivors and studied the ways in which the environment, and especially trauma, could leave a chemical mark on a person's genes that is passed down to the next generation. That empirical research emphasized the major role that stress hormones play in how the brain develops, and thus in the biological mechanisms by which trauma is transmitted from generation to generation.

A large body of research done at the Icahn School of Medicine at Mount Sinai Hospital by Dr. Rachel Yehuda, director of traumatic stress studies, and her team reveals that the offspring of Holocaust survivors have lower levels of cortisol, a hormone that helps the body bounce back after trauma. It was found that descendants of people who survived the Holocaust have different stress-hormone profiles than their peers, perhaps predisposing them to anxiety disorders. Research indicates that healthy offspring of Holocaust survivors as well as of enslaved people, of war veterans, and of parents who experienced major trauma are more likely to present symptoms of PTSD after traumatic events or after witnessing a violent incident.

From an evolutionary perspective, the purpose of those kinds of epigenetic changes might be to biologically prepare children for an environment similar to that of their parents and help them survive, but in fact they often leave them more vulnerable to carrying symptoms of trauma that they didn't experience firsthand.

This research is not surprising for those of us who study the human mind. In our clinical work we see how traumatic experience invades the psyche of the next generation and shows itself in uncanny and often surprising ways. The people we love and those who raised us live inside us; we experience their emotional pain, we dream their memories, we know what was not explicitly conveyed to us, and these things shape our lives in ways that we don't always understand.

We inherit family traumas, even those that we haven't been told about. Working in Paris with Holocaust survivors and their children, the Hungarian-born psychoanalysts Maria Torok and Nicolas Abraham used the word "phantom" to describe the many ways in which the second generation felt their parents' devastation and losses, even when the parents never talked about them. Their inherited feelings of the parents' unprocessed trauma were the phantoms that lived inside them, the ghosts of the unsaid and the unspeakable.

It is those "ghostly" experiences, not quite alive but also not dead, that we inherit. They invade our reality in visible and actual ways; they loom in, leaving traces. We know and feel things and we don't always recognize their source.

Emotional Inheritance interweaves my patients' narratives and my own personal stories of love and loss, personal and national trauma, with a psychoanalytic lens and the most recent psychological research. It describes the many ways in which we can locate the ghosts of the past that hold us back and interfere with our lives. Everything we do not consciously know is relived. It is held in our minds and in our bodies and makes itself known to us via what we call symptoms: headaches, obsessions, phobias, insomnia, can all be signs of what we have pushed away to the darkest recesses of our minds.

How do we inherit, hold, and process things that we don't remember or didn't experience ourselves? What is the weight of that which is present but not fully known? Can we really keep secrets from one another, and what do we pass on to the next generation?

Those and other questions are explored on the path to setting free the parts of ourselves kept in captivity by the secrets of the past.

THIS BOOK WAS born on the couch, in the intimate dialogue between my patients and me. With their permission, it introduces their emotional inheritance, unthinkable trauma, and hidden truths, as well as my own, as we move beyond the legacy of trauma. I explore feelings that are forbidden, memories that our minds forget or trivialize, and pieces of our history that our loyalty to those we love doesn't always allow us to truly know or remember. Each story presents its own unique way of examining the past while looking forward to the future. When we are ready to unpack our inheritance, we are able to confront the ghosts we carry within.

In the book, I describe the many faces of inherited trauma, its impact, and how we move forward. Part I focuses on the third generation of survivors: a grandparent's trauma as it presents itself in the grandchild's mind. I look into the secrets of forbidden love, at infidelity and its relation to intergenerational trauma. I investigate the ghosts of sexual abuse, the effects of suicide on the next generations, and the remnants of homophobia in the unconscious mind. I discuss Professor Yolanda Gampel's idea of "the radioactivity of trauma," which is the emotional "radiation" of disaster that spreads into the lives of the generations that follow.

Part II focuses on our parents' buried secrets. It explores unspeakable truths from the time before we were born or from our infancy. Those truths, although not consciously known to us, shape our lives. I discuss how one can become frozen from the loss of a sibling, I introduce the idea of "unwelcome" babies and their death wish as adults, and I analyze a soldier's trauma and masculine vulnerability as revealed in the therapeutic relationship.

Part III searches for the secrets we keep from ourselves, the realities that are too threatening to know or that we can't fully process. These are stories of motherhood, of loyalties and lies, physical abuse, friendship and painful loss, demonstrating how often something is, in fact, known to us even as it is kept in a hidden place in our minds.

The secrets we keep from ourselves are meant to protect us by distorting reality and to help us hold unpleasant information far from our consciousness. In order to do that, we use our defense mechanisms: we idealize those we don't want to feel ambivalent about, identify with the parent who abused us, split the world into good and bad in order to organize the world as safe and predictable. We project into the other what we don't want to feel or what makes us too anxious to know about ourselves.

It is the emotional defense mechanism of repression that trivializes our memories and strips them of meaning. Repression protects us by splitting a memory from its emotional significance. In those cases, the trauma is held in the mind as an event that is "not a big deal," "nothing important." The disconnect between ideas and feelings allows us to protect ourselves from feeling something too devastating but also keeps the trauma isolated and unprocessed.

Our defenses are important for our mental health. They manage our emotional pain and design our perception of ourselves and of the world around us. Their protective function, however, also limits our ability to examine our lives and live them to the fullest. Those experiences that were too painful for us to entirely grasp and process are the ones that are passed down to the next generation. It is those traumas that are unspeakable and too painful for the mind to digest that become our own inheritance and impact our offspring, and their offspring, in ways they cannot understand or control.

Most of the personal stories that I tell here are accounts of buried traumas from the past that were held silently between people, life events that were not fully conveyed but still were known by others in cryptic ways. It is the stories that have never been told, the sounds that have often been muted, that leave us undone. I invite you to come with me to break the silence, to trace and discover the ghosts that limit our freedom, the emotional inheritance that prevents us from following our dreams, from creating, loving, and living to our full potential.

PART I

OUR GRANDPARENTS

Inherited Trauma in Past Generations

WE ALL HAVE our phantoms. But as the psychoanalysts Maria Torok and Nicolas Abraham once wrote, "What haunts are not the dead, but the gaps left within us by the secrets of others." They were referring to intergenerational secrets and unprocessed experiences that very often don't have a voice or an image associated with them but loom in our minds nonetheless. We carry emotional material that belongs to our parents and grandparents, retaining losses of theirs that they never fully articulated. We feel these traumas even if we don't consciously know them. Old family secrets live inside us.

This section focuses primarily on the third generation of survivors. It turns a lens on the aftermath of the

Holocaust, where repressed trauma often turns into name-less dread and untold stories are reenacted again and again. It explores the effects of early loss on the next generations, looks into the ways a grandparent's sexual abuse might impact their grandchild's life, and presents the secrets of a grandfather's forbidden love as they appear in a grandson's mind. When set against a backdrop of life and death, it is sometimes the erotic that offers a lifeline, a way into the land of the living. That which we don't have permission to know haunts us and remains mystified, rendering us inconsolable.

1

LIFE AND DEATH
IN LOVE AFFAIRS

EVE DRIVES AN hour, twice a week, to get to her session with me. She tells me that she hates driving, and how much she wishes someone would drive her, wait for her outside my office, and then drive her back home. She doesn't need that person to entertain her; they don't even need to talk. It would be more than enough for her to just sit next to the driver and listen to the music in the background.

I feel a wave of sadness listening to Eve describing herself sitting silently next to the driver. I picture the little girl she used to be, trying to be good and quiet, not to interrupt anyone, not to get in trouble, pretending she doesn't exist.

I asked her in one of our first sessions what her earliest childhood memory was. She said, "I was five years old, waiting outside school for my mother to pick me up, and she forgot. I figured that I had to sit there and wait until my mother remembered. 'Be patient,' I told myself."

A first childhood memory often conceals within it the main ingredients of future therapy. It frequently illustrates the reasons the patient seeks therapy, and portrays a picture of the patient's view of herself. Every memory hides within it previous and also subsequent repressed memories.

Eve's first memory conveys to me the experience of being forgotten. Slowly it becomes clear that she was often left alone with no parental supervision and that she grew up, the oldest of four children, in a family where there was much neglect and emotional deadness.

I feel drawn to Eve. She is in her forties, her long brunette hair flowing onto her shoulders, her green eyes usually covered with big dark sunglasses. Eve takes off her sunglasses as she walks into the room, then quickly sits on the couch. She greets me with a shy smile, and I notice the dimple on her right cheek. She takes off her high heels and stays barefoot, sitting crossed legged on the couch. Eve is beautiful, and in some moments, when looking at me with the eyes of a young girl, she seems lost.

I wonder if Eve's mother eventually picked her up, and I try to imagine how Eve felt waiting there for her, hiding her fear that her mother might never come.

I ask, but Eve is silent. She doesn't remember. In our sessions, she often becomes dissociative, gazing out the window as if she is with me but also not with me. Something about her is breathtaking, but at times she seems flat.

Eve is frequently distant; she is careful about expressing intense emotion, and she lapses into long silences.

I look at her and wonder if I, too, am assigned to be her driver, a grown-up in her life, someone who will be there on time, take control, and drive her to where she needs to be. I sit quietly, aware that it might take a while for her to look at me or say anything.

"I was with him again last night," she opens the session, referring to her lover, Josh, whom she sees a few times a week.

Around 8 p.m. when his colleagues leave, he opens Line, the Japanese app they use to text each other, and sends her a message to come to his office. Eve explains to me that they needed a safe way to communicate.

"When Josh first suggested we use this app, I thought he said 'Lying' instead of 'Line,' and I said to myself, 'What a strangely inappropriate name for an app.'" She laughs and then adds sarcastically, "I think there should be a network for cheaters, maybe a chat room where they share information and give each other advice, like the groups they have for new mothers. Someone should have made a business out of it, don't you think? Millions of people are lost and confused, not sure how to survive adultery." She smiles but seems sadder than ever.

She doesn't look at me. "Josh and I bought a membership to SoulCycle as an alibi for meeting each other in the evenings. It's a good excuse to come home sweaty and go right into the shower." She pauses and adds, "Washing his smell off my body always makes me sad. I would rather go to sleep with it."

Eve takes a breath, as if she is trying to calm herself, and then adds with a smile, "Josh thinks SoulCycle can make money from selling an 'alibi package,' where people can buy false memberships at a discount price."

I smile back, even as I know that none of this is funny. There is so much confusion, guilt, and fear in her witty way of telling me things. Suddenly she is fully present and I feel the intensity of her pain. She is alive, I think, and I wonder out loud if she wants to say more about her love affair.

During our first session Eve told me that she was married and had two children. Her daughter had just turned twelve and her son was nine. She told me she had decided to start therapy because something terrible had happened, something that made her realize she needed help. Then she told me about Josh.

Eve spends a few evenings a week in Josh's office. Josh is a creature of habit and they have a routine: first they have sex, then they order food, and when they have finished eating he drives her home.

Eve tells me about their sex, first hesitantly and then in detail.

"With Josh, nothing is in my control," she says, looking to see if I understand what she means. She explains that in her submission to him she feels held. She feels that he knows everything about her and about her body, and that she can lose control under his domination.

"He brings me back to life, do you know what I mean?" She doesn't wait for an answer.

Life and death, from the start, are strong forces in Eve's narrative. We begin exploring the links between sex, death and reparation, and the uncanny ways these are related to Eve's family history. Her mother, I learn, had lost her own mother to cancer when she was fourteen years old. For two years Eve's mother took care of her dying mother but a part of her died with her. Eve and I will slowly realize how through sexual submission she gets in touch with her longing to be taken care of, to stay alive and to repair a traumatic past.

Eve looks at her watch and starts putting on her shoes, preparing for the end of the session. Then she leans back and says quietly:

"When we are done and Josh drives me home, I become emotional. I love having sex with him and I love when he drives me."

There is another moment of silence, and she says, almost

whispering, "I look at him holding the steering wheel, a serious look on his face, and I think that he is the most handsome man I have ever met. And I want to kiss him but I know it's not a good idea; after all, we are not in his office anymore, and we make believe that he is my car-service driver.

"He drops me off a few blocks from my building, and when I say good night my heart breaks a little. I really don't want to go upstairs, back into the highway of my life. Josh knows exactly how I feel, and without me needing to say anything, he tells me, 'Don't forget how much I love you. I'll see you on Wednesday. It's very soon; it's sooner than you think.'

"I make a face and he knows that I think Wednesday is years from now and that I will have so many feelings and thoughts that he won't be a part of until Wednesday, and he says, 'I'm on our app. I'm here, even if I'm not physically with you.'"

She puts on her sunglasses. "This is usually when I stop feeling anything and leave the car." I see that she becomes disconnected in order to leave him, and that she does it again right before my eyes as she tells me about it. I lose her to a long silence before she leaves.

MANY OF MY patients come to see me because of my professional writing and teaching on the subject of sexuality.

I see men and women who feel destroyed by a partner's affair, others who had or are having affairs, and those who are lovers of married people. Their stories are different and their motivations are diverse, but all these people reveal themselves to be tortured as they struggle with their own secrets or with the secrets of the people in their lives.

While I am aware of the transactional aspect of every relationship, I also believe in love. I believe in the power of attachment between two people, in loyalty as one of the basic foundations of trust, and I consider destructive and creative forces to be part of every relationship. We love and at times we also hate the people we love; we trust them but are also afraid of the injuries and hurt they might cause us. One of the goals associated with growth is the ability to integrate positive and negative feelings: to hate lovingly, to love while recognizing moments of disappointment and anger. The more we can know and own our destructive urges, the more able we become to love fully.

Life, to some degree, is always about that tension between the wish to destroy — ruin the love, goodness, and life itself — and Eros, which represents not only sex, but also the urge to survive, create, produce, and love. That tension exists in every aspect of our lives, including in our relationships.

Psychological awareness helps us to identify and bring those urges and wishes into consciousness, and to question our choices and the choices of the people who came before us. When it comes to affairs, that work is multilayered, and the distinction between destruction and death, and survival and life isn't always obvious.

One significant reason why people come to therapy is to search for unknown truths about themselves. That investigation starts with a wish to know who we truly are and who our parents were, and it always includes the dread of knowing. Why does Eve have this relationship with Josh? Why now? What part of it is about a need to survive and bring herself back to life, and what part is attached to death and destruction? In what way is her present life a reflection of the lives of the women who came before and an attempt to heal not only herself, but also her wounded mother and her dying grandmother?

Infidelity is destructive in the sense that it always causes damage to a relationship, even if that damage is at first invisible. But people have affairs not only because they want to destroy or get out of their relationships; paradoxically, infidelity is sometimes an effort to stay in a marriage. Cheating is often a way to balance power in the relationship or to fulfill needs that are not met. In many cases, while the affair is a sexual acting out and an indirect way to express negative feelings like hostility and anger, it is also a way to protect the marriage from those feelings while maintaining a status quo within the relationship.

Through sex, feelings that are not allowed in the relationship itself, particularly aggression, find their expression. It is not unusual for people to describe sex outside the marriage as more aggressive, and sex in the marriage as more gentle and "civilized." As partners unconsciously protect each other from aggression, they numb the relationship. When there is no room for aggression, there is usually no sex either.

The same dialectic tension between life and death exists in sexual desire and especially in long-term relationships. In his book *Can Love Last?*, American psychoanalyst Stephen A. Mitchell discusses the clash between adventure and security in sexual life. Mitchell emphasizes that romance, vitality, and sexuality are factors that make one's life not only worth living but also worth cultivating and savoring. Romance, he suggests, has a great deal to do with an existential excitement about being alive. Over time, sexual romance easily degrades into something much less enlivening or maybe even deadening, because it thrives on danger, mystery, and adventure, not the safety and familiarity of a long-term relationship.

Can we continue to desire the people we feel most safe with? Mitchell asks. He suggests that it is the delicate balance between security and danger, the familiar and the novel, that is the secret for long-term love. In her innovative book *Mating in Captivity*, psychotherapist Esther

Perel elaborates on that paradox of domesticity and sexual desire and works to help couples open a playful space for adventure and therefore sexual excitement in their relationships. Perel further develops those themes and others to examine the complexity of infidelity.

A psychoanalytic investigation is a complex and nuanced journey into one's delicate heart. Danger and security, destruction and construction, life and death, and the plight of multiple generations appear, in different ways, in each and every one of those journeys.

During our first session together, Eve doesn't take off her sunglasses. She sits on the couch with her legs crossed and sobs.

"I messed up my life," she says. "I don't know, maybe I already destroyed it. I'm not sure what to do."

She tells me that her husband is a good man and that she has a satisfying marriage.

"I actually love my husband," she says. "We have such a sweet family, my kids are so wonderful, and they are everything I have always dreamed of. I have everything I wanted and maybe I'm just too greedy." She then tells me about the night that made her realize that she had lost control of her life.

"We usually meet in his office, but that weekend was different because both his wife and my husband were away, and we thought it was a good opportunity for us to spend the night together. We never did that before and I think both of us were excited but also anxious."

She asked her babysitter to stay the night with the kids, and Josh reserved a room in a hotel across the street from his office. Eve tells me that if her husband looks at the app where they can see each other's location, he could easily find her. They had installed the app earlier in the year so they could keep track of their daughter, who had just turned twelve and had started walking to school on her own.

"The app became a huge problem, as I was aware that my family could always see where I was. I know this doesn't sound believable, but I really hate lying," she says, almost apologizing. "I would rather not give any explanation than to have to lie. I decided to turn my phone off that night, so I wouldn't have to lie about where I was." She sighs. "Oh God. What a mess."

Eve pauses, tears in her eyes.

"My night with Josh was even better than I had imagined it would be. It is hard to put into words how I felt because I didn't know a feeling like that even existed. We were finally in a peaceful place, just the two of us, and we had what seemed like an endless amount of time. It felt like we were a real couple, completely devoted to each other, completely in each other's bodies and minds. We had sex for hours and I kept whispering in Josh's ear, 'I love you. You make me so, so happy.'

"'I know, baby, I'm happy too,' he said.

"'Do you think we can make this place our home?' I asked him, referring to the small hotel room that seemed so perfect in that moment." Eve lifts her head and looks at me, "As I tell you this now, I realize that I just projected all my wishes on that stupid hotel room. I feel like such an idiot. When we were lying down and I put my head on his shoulder, I didn't think about anything. Nothing else existed in the moment. I was truly happy."

Eve pauses briefly. She doesn't look at me and continues. "There is something unusual about being in Josh's arms. Something about his touch. It's like he is both strong and gentle at the same time and I feel that I totally lose myself when I'm with him. It's a feeling I've never had before. But I guess that was the problem. That's why the night ended so badly." She sighs.

"I woke up at 6 a.m. and when I left the hotel I turned on my phone. I had ten voice mails and many texts from the babysitter saying that my son had had an asthma attack and that they were at the hospital. I started sobbing, trying to reach the doctor on the phone. I just couldn't believe that I had let that happen. That was the moment when I realized that I had lost control of my life and was in big trouble. That's when I decided to see a therapist." She turns to me and asks in a desperate tone, "What am I going to do? Tell me. Is it crazy that I love him?"

Freud wrote that one of his least favorite things to do was to work with patients who were in love. For Freud, love was an irrational feeling and the person in love was in a semi-psychotic phase, out of touch with reality. He believed that this phase did not allow the patient to be in touch with any emotional reality other than their love and erotic feelings, and thus genuine awareness was almost impossible.

Irvin Yalom opens his book *Love's Executioner* by saying that he, too, doesn't like to work with patients who are in love. He assumes this is because of envy. "I, too, crave enchantment," he writes with honesty.

No doubt the therapist, almost like the child who peeks into his parents' bedroom, is an "outsider" witness of his patient's love affair and might feel left out and jealous. However, the therapist doesn't identify only with the excluded outsider, meaning the child, but also with the insiders, the ones who fall in love.

It becomes more complicated, though, when that love is an illicit one and when there are many moral and ethical components to it. Like most people, therapists can have many feelings about that kind of love; they can have a moral conflict, feel guilty, or identify with the betrayed partner; they can feel envious of the patient who is able to do something they themselves may want to do; they might want to make the patient a "better person" and help him or her end the affair; they may even have a romantic fantasy about the patient running away with her lover.

I sit with that complexity as I listen to Eve, aware that the search for truth is always painful. It forces us to slow down and examine our lives, to replace action with reflection. What is the real meaning of an affair? Can Eve tolerate knowing the forces behind her infidelity? Can she bear recognizing the pain she carries from childhood and that her affair promises to soothe? Can she identify the ways her mother and grandmother both live in her love affair? Will she be able to survive?

EVE ARRIVES FIVE minutes late to our next session.

"I woke up late and hardly made it here," she says as she walks in. "There was so much traffic and I couldn't find parking. I thought, 'I need a miracle to make it.'"

I listen to her and wonder if she wishes she hadn't made it to my office so she wouldn't have to start the painful process of self-reflection. But I also hear her surprise about the fact that she actually made it, not just to our session, but maybe also to her life.

"It might be surprising to you that you made it to where you are — becoming a functioning adult with a successful career, with a loving husband and two children — maybe it seems like a miracle," I say.

She smiles. "Sometimes I'm not really sure how that

happened. I can't believe that this is actually my life. I know it might sound superficial, but even the way I look surprises me sometimes," she says. "I was an ugly little girl, 'strange-looking,' as my parents used to say." She looks at me and adds, "But the truth is that now I don't know anything anymore. I feel like I'm turning myself back into the girl I used to be, the girl who had nothing and no one. I feel that I destroyed everything that I created and that I won't have a second chance. This time I won't make it."

Eve doesn't remember much from her childhood. She remembers being alone a lot, playing by herself under the desk in the bedroom she shared with her three younger brothers. She used to make little people out of paper and play family with them. They were the big family she hoped she would have one day, a family with many children who love and protect her and one another. The space under the desk was their home and she covered it with a blanket and hid there so she could play her imaginary games without interruptions.

"There was one scene I used to play again and again," she tells me.

"It was the girl's birthday and none of the family members would say 'Happy Birthday' to her. They ignored her, insulted and attacked her. It was the worst day of her life and she would sit in the corner of the house and cry silently."

The scene always ended with a transformation: suddenly, in one minute, everything changed. The rejected girl discovered that it was all a mistake, a way for the family to hide a big surprise party that they had planned for her.

"She realizes that it was just a trick," Eve says in a childish tone, and I know she is telling me about how as a child she hoped it would all end up being a mistake, how she wished everything would change one day. The wish for transformation was an important part of her childhood fantasy. She dreamed of how she was going to transform her ugliness into beauty, her desperation into hope, her helplessness into power, hate into love, and everything that felt dead into life. And it happened. The little girl was transformed into a beautiful, powerful, and successful woman. She created the family she'd always wanted. But when her daughter was twelve years old, she suddenly felt empty, as if she were dying inside.

"And then I met Josh," she says. She is silent for a moment, turns, and gazes out the window. "He takes care of me as if I were a little girl," she says quietly, as if talking to herself. "He takes care of me the way no one ever did, the way I imagine my mother took care of her mother."

I follow Eve's associations and walk with her into her family history, into the bedroom where her sick grandmother lay, Eve's mother, Sara, then twelve years old, lying next to her. I note that this is the exact age of Eve's daughter when her affair with Josh began.

Eve's grandmother had been sick with liver cancer for two years. She went through radiation treatment and chemotherapy and was in a short remission, and then the cancer came back. She suffered through more rounds of chemo but only became sicker and sicker. Sara was fourteen years old when her mother died.

"My mother, like me, was the oldest of four children and the only girl. She was her mother's main caretaker and a responsible and devoted daughter. She told me that for months her mother would lie in bed all day with a high fever, and she would try to help, bringing her ice and wet towels to control the fever. But nothing worked. As time passed the fevers started earlier in the day and lasted all night. My grandfather moved to sleep in the living room; my mother would wake up in the middle of the night to check on her mother and would run home after school to see if she needed anything.

"In the last few weeks her mother hardly opened her eyes. When she did, it seemed like she was staring into space, not really able to see anything. My mother wasn't sure if her mother even knew she was lying next to her anymore. Her skin became yellow and her mouth was a little open all the time, as if she couldn't hold it closed. As toxins from the liver went into her brain she became confused and once in a while whispered something that didn't make any sense, for instance, that they needed to feed the dogs, but they never had dogs. My mother wondered if she was referring to a dog she'd had as a child, but she never knew if that dog existed.

"I don't think she ever got over her mother's death," Eve says. "She told me about the last days of her mother's life many times, as if telling me would help her process it better or as if she needed me to know every detail so she wouldn't feel so alone."

In the last few days of her mother's life, Sara didn't go to school. She would crawl into bed with her mother and try to listen to her breathing. It comforted her to know that her mother was still alive, that her mother could hear her. But Sara knew she couldn't touch her mother anymore; her body had become so sensitive, even a gentle touch could hurt her.

A nurse from the hospital came to visit their house every day, and one day she called Sara to the other room and told her that her mother was going to die soon, in weeks or maybe days. She gave her a little green book that described what to expect. But Sara didn't really believe it. She thought that if she stayed in bed with her mother, she could keep her alive; that if she made sure she synchronized her breaths with her mother's, they would breathe together forever.

On Sara's fourteenth birthday, her mother took seven deep breaths, each of them sounding like a sigh, and then one last breath. She had a little smile on her face, but she wasn't alive anymore.

Eve tells me this as if she is telling me about her own dead mother. I have tears in my eyes but she doesn't. She looks at me and takes a deep breath herself. Is she making sure she is still alive?

She moves uncomfortably. "You mentioned before that my mother was twelve years old when her mother got sick, and my daughter was twelve years old when I started seeing Josh. I never made that connection. When we have sex I always cry. Once in a while I ask him to save my life, to take me somewhere, drive me far away."

"It is not unusual for sex to become a desperate attempt to heal our wounded parents and ourselves," I say, and Eve starts to cry.

"It's so awful," she whispers. "If mothers get sick when their daughters are twelve years old, and then they die, then of course I had to save my life," she says. I ask if she has a memory from that age, from when she was around twelve years old.

Eve looks at me, surprised. She doesn't have many childhood memories.

"How strange," she says. "After all, my mother was the one who raised me, the one who was home with the kids,

37

but I don't have any real memories of times with her." She pauses and gazes out the window. I feel that she is suddenly gone again and I wait silently for her to come back. It is in that moment that I identify the relationship between her moments of numbness, her grandmother's death, and the impact this had on her mother.

I hear myself asking, "Is your mother alive?"

Eve looks startled. We both know that I would have known if her mother, Sara, had died — she would have told me — but still I asked. My question implies that her mother is in some ways dead, that she died there in that bedroom with her own mother and could never be a functional mother herself.

"I suddenly remember something," Eve says. "When you asked me just now if my mother was alive, I had the most disturbing image from my childhood. I'm not even sure how it is related. An image of a dead dog.

"When I was twelve years old I found a little puppy in the street, right near our house. I petted it, and when I put it back in the street and turned to go home, the puppy followed me. I remember feeling so happy. I felt that the puppy loved me and I picked it up again and decided to take the chance and bring it home. I knew my mother wouldn't be happy about it — she never wanted to have pets in the house — but I made up my mind to do anything to convince her to adopt this puppy.

"I remember walking into the house, giving the puppy some water that I poured into a glass, and looking for my mother. She was in bed. When I'm thinking about it now, she was always in bed," Eve says. "Ha, I never thought about it," she adds, and continues. "I sat next to her in the bed and whispered, 'Mom, I found a puppy.'"

I listen to Eve and remember the dogs her grandmother mentioned before she died. Eve continues.

"My mother didn't open her eyes and just mumbled, 'What do you mean you found it?'

"I said, 'It followed me on the street and I felt bad leaving it there alone. I thought we could take care of this puppy and — '

"My mom stopped me; her eyes were still closed. 'We won't,' she said firmly. 'Bring it back to where you found it.'

"'But, Mom' — I started to cry — 'I can't. The puppy doesn't have parents; she doesn't have anyone to take care of her. I promise you, you won't have to do anything. I will do everything. I'll take care of it myself. Please, Mom, please.'

"My mother opened her eyes.

"'Eve, don't make me angry,' she said. 'Did you hear what I just said? Bring it back to where you found it. We won't have dogs in this house.'"

Eve looks devastated. She starts to sob. "I had no choice and took the dog outside and left it on the street. The next day I found the puppy dead across the street from our building. Someone told me that she was hit by a car. I thought it was all because she tried to follow me back home."

Eve is weeping and I try to hold back my own tears. I feel her anger and helplessness as she identifies with the abandoned puppy, who, like her mother, doesn't have a mother, doesn't have anyone to take care of her. That dog, which was thrown back to the street, was also like herself as a child, abandoned again and again, walking alone in the world, and hoping that someone would adopt her and transform her life.

The dead dog represented all the deadness Eve carried inside her: her dead grandmother, her traumatized and emotionally dead mother, and her dead self.

The French psychoanalyst André Green coined the term "dead mother," referring to an unavailable, usually depressed, and emotionally absent mother. Green described a traumatized mother who is distanced and emotionally dead. He explained that it was usually loss that caused the mother to die emotionally, and that the child then became invested for the rest of her life in trying to connect to the mother, in an attempt to revive and bring her back to life. Any child whose most devastating fear is abandonment will insist on connecting with their mother and do anything to feel close to her, including compromising parts of themselves. When they give up on bringing her back to life, they will try to restore the connection through the renunciation of their own aliveness. They will meet the mother in her deadness and thus will develop their own emotional deadness.

The intergenerational aspect of deadness is everywhere in Eve's psyche. She carries that emotional inheritance and identifies with her dead mother. Deep inside she, too, feels broken, deadened, ashamed. As a child, she tried to transform that feeling in the moments when she dreamed about creating life, about becoming a mother, having a hundred children. She calculated that if she gave birth ten times and each time she had ten babies, then a hundred kids could be a pretty realistic number of children. They would be like a family of puppies, snuggling together. She fantasized about a life filled with love, as she was struggling with layers of death.

The wish for reparation colored Eve's sexual desire. Sex served as a way to actively bring herself into the heart of her family trauma. Through the act of sex, we can touch the abyss, our sorrow, our desperation.

"I need Josh to pin me down. And then I want him to touch me, gently, all over," Eve tells me. "I want him to hold me as tight as he can, tie me to the bed so I can't move, so he has all the power and I have no other choice but to trust him to treat my soul with care. I want him to make me feel better."

Eve had sex with Josh, looked death in the eye, and fought it. She insisted that this time she would win, this time she would fix all the damage and the humiliation, she would revive and repair the deadness in herself, in her past, in her present, and certainly in her future. Her unconscious fantasy was that everything would be reparable and forgivable and she could end the cycle and stay fully alive as her daughter turned twelve.

Reparation is an impulse of Eros, of life. It is the strongest element of creativity and is based on the wish to fix the damage and to heal the people we love. Therefore it creates hope and helps one feel more alive and mourn one's losses. "Manic reparation" is a form of reparation that is more defensive than productive. It is action oriented and endlessly repeated, and it never achieves its goal because it aims for triumph and absolute repair. It ignores the fact that there are no new complete beginnings and that forgiveness and recovery include pain.

Josh could not repair the losses in Eve's life. In fact, every time they said goodbye she felt helpless and relived those losses. In therapy Eve realizes that the exact battle she believed she was winning was a form of repetition of the past she was trying to avoid. She became aware that the same thing she thought was saving her life in fact made her an absent and dead mother to her own children, and so instead of repairing her history she was repeating it.

When she realized that her son could have died, she had to stop the manic cycle and face reality, the painful truth that what has been done cannot be fully undone; it can only be processed and mourned.

At the end of our session, Eve puts on her shoes, opens her bag, and grabs her keys, but she doesn't put her glasses on right away. Instead, she sits a minute in silence and then smiles.

"You know, I think I'm actually looking forward to driving myself today. I'm not sure why I never realized this before: that being the driver means I can choose where to go. I can go home. Or not. It's up to me."

I watch Eve as she leaves my office, feeling hopeful for her for the first time since we met.

2

CONFUSION OF TONGUES

I'M NOT SURPRISED when I get an email from Lara, who was my patient nineteen years ago. Lara was only ten years old when her parents suddenly ended her treatment and moved the family to the West Coast. In the years since, I have thought about her often, remembering her unusual story, wondering how she is doing. When I see her name in my inbox it is almost as if I am expecting it.

"I'm writing to see if we could meet," Lara writes. "I'm twenty-nine years old now and there is so much I would like to talk to you about. Do you even remember me?"

It is hard not to remember Lara. She was one of my first child patients when I opened my private practice in New York City. I saw her for two years and often felt uneasy thinking about her unresolved family situation, which I have revisited in my head over all these years.

Lara's was one of the most confusing cases of sexual

abuse that I have treated, and as time passed and I studied the nature of the intergenerational aspect of sexual abuse, I felt that I was able to make better sense of it. Maybe it was my ongoing desire to share those thoughts with Lara that made me hope that she would contact me.

I was researching the topic of sexual abuse in childhood when I started seeing Lara.

Beatrice Beebe, one of my mentors and an infant researcher at Columbia University, is known for saying "Research is me-search." By that she means that all psychological research, even when we are not aware of it, is our quest to understand and heal ourselves and the people who raised us.

Starting this research, I was not sure what I was looking for. What was it that I really needed to know about myself and about the world around me? What was my "me-search"?

That is the question I have asked every student I have mentored since, with the genuine belief that deep inside we continuously try to resolve the mysteries of our own minds. Feelings are always the motivations for intellectual investigations, even as we rationalize the world around us.

I started my research interested in what the Hungarian psychoanalyst Sándor Ferenczi called "the confusion of tongues." Borrowing from the biblical story of the Tower of Babel, Ferenczi refers to the confusion between the language of tenderness that children speak and the language of passion that abusers introduce. The paradox of affection and exploitation is one of the most prevalent confusions related to sexual abuse, one that leaves children bewildered and tormented. Abusers don't just threaten and scare children; they often provide affection, promise security, and make the child feel special. I focused my research on what children's play could teach us about their emotional experiences and vulnerabilities, and I was particularly interested in documenting the playing out with children of fairy tales, stories that contain emotional material that carries universal meaning. I chose one fairy tale to research with my young patients: "Little Red Riding Hood."

About a week after my research proposal was approved, Lara walked into my office. She opened the session by saying, "Today I have an idea of what we could do."

She and I usually played "family" together. She would ask me to play the daughter so she could be the mother, and through that role-play I not only learned but also felt how painful it was to be a daughter in her family. Playing a daughter who, like herself, lived with her parents, Hanna and Jed, and with her half brother, Ethan, who was nine years older, allowed me to know what no one could tell me in words: that they were all confused and scared and that Lara was holding a family secret for all of them.

"What is your idea?" I asked, and Lara surprised me with the answer: "Can we play Red Riding Hood together?"

I was stunned by the coincidence. How did she know that this was the fairy tale I had chosen for my research and that I had gotten the approval to start only the week before?

The more experience I have with patients, the more I learn how unconsciously connected we are to the people around us. With Lara, it was the first time I'd experienced that, but it wouldn't be the last. Since then I have had many uncanny coincidences with my patients. Through our dreams, reveries, and synchronicities we realize that we know more about one another than we are aware of.

Lara smiled. "You are the daughter and I am the mother," she said.

I opened the closet. There were the new puppets I had just gotten: a girl with a red dress, a mother, a grandmother, and a wolf.

"What about the grandmother and the wolf?" I asked. "Who plays them?"

Lara paused. "We don't need a wolf," she said. "There are no wolves in our story."

A FEW WEEKS before my first session with Lara, I had met with her parents, Hanna and Jed.

When working with children I always meet first with

the parents, to gather information about the child and the family and to discuss the goals and process of therapy. Although the child is the one in therapy, very often it is the parents who need the most help. Children frequently express the reality of the family and become what we call the "identified patient," which means the one who seems like the "sick" member of the family. Those children usually carry and express the problems of the whole family as a unit. Most families have one member who is unconsciously assigned to carry the symptoms, that is, the family member on whom the family projects the pathology. That person, often one of the children, will be the one sent to therapy. When treating families as a system, we explore the role of the child as the symptom carrier for the family.

Lara was the "identified patient" in her family. She was in second grade and would wake up in the mornings nauseous, holding her stomach and crying that she didn't want to go to school. Her parents believed she suffered from social anxiety. After meeting with Lara, I understood her anxiety a little differently, realizing that she was worried about her mother, and therefore it was hard for her to separate from her. It wasn't that Lara didn't want to go to school, but rather that she wanted to stay home with Hanna, whom she experienced as distressed and felt she needed to protect.

During that first session, Hanna and Jed told me an unusual and frightening story. They explained that when Lara was only five years old, her grandmother, Hanna's mother, Masha, filed a complaint against Ethan, Jed's son from his first marriage, for molesting Lara. Ethan was fourteen years old then, and social services were called to the house to investigate. But no signs of sexual abuse were found and the file was closed. Since then, Masha had filed eight more complaints against Ethan. Each time there was an investigation but no evidence was found and no charges were filed.

"Our family is torn. We don't know what to do and whom to believe," Hanna told me during that first session. "I haven't slept well since it happened."

Jed looked at Hanna and told me that Hanna was the one who had raised Ethan. Jed's first wife had died when Ethan was only seven years old, and when Hanna had married Jed, she had become a mother to his son. Hanna loved Ethan.

"Since her mother accused Ethan of molesting Lara, everything in our family has changed," Jed said. "We all became suspicious of one another, not sure who lies and whom to believe, whom we need to protect and whom to blame."

Hanna started to cry. "I don't believe he did it," she said. "I really don't believe it. I know him so well and I know my mother; when it comes to these things she can be a little crazy."

"What are 'these things'?" I asked.

Jed reached out and held Hanna's hand. She didn't answer.

"This situation has created a lot of tension between us," he said. "Hanna became depressed. She blames herself."

"What are you blaming yourself for?" I asked.

"I'm her mother," Hanna said, sobbing. "I'm the one who should know what the truth is." She grabbed a tissue from the box and looked at me. "I don't know, maybe I'm wrong and my mother is right and something terrible happened right in front of my eyes. I don't know how to protect my daughter."

There was a long silence and then Hanna said, "I realize that maybe it's my mother that I should protect my daughter from. My own mother, whom I love. But why would she blame him? Why would she do that?"

Hanna and Jed hoped that someone would tell them what had really happened. They yearned for the truth.

"What does Lara know about this situation? Is she aware of anything?" I asked before we ended the session.

Jed looked at Hanna and they were both silent for a long minute.

"About a year ago, my mother came to visit and told Lara that Ethan had sexually abused her." Hanna sighed.

"She told Lara that all those years she had been trying to help her, 'to scream her scream' she called it. But that no one listened to her. She told her that she should never be alone with Ethan."

Jed nodded. "From then on, Lara didn't want to go to school anymore. We thought she had become afraid of people and that's why we decided to bring her to therapy."

The first session ended and my head was spinning. I felt nauseous and realized that those were exactly the symptoms Lara's parents described Lara as having. I was curious to meet her.

The next day Lara arrived at her first session accompanied by Jed. She held her father's hand, her long black hair tied in a ponytail, and didn't look at me.

"I like your office," she said quietly, looking around, a shy smile on her face. I liked Lara from the first moment.

In that initial session, Lara told me about her family and described nonchalantly how Ethan was accused of touching her inappropriately.

"My grandmother doesn't like my brother," she said. "Maybe she even hates him and she wants him to go to jail."

Lara talked about these facts without emotion, as if none of this was about her. She turned to look at the dolls in the corner of the room and asked if she could play with them.

For a year, during every session we played while we talked. I observed the play and tried to listen to what she was teaching me about her world, her emotional experience, and her vulnerabilities.

Since it was not clear whether Lara had in fact been sexually abused, I decided not to include her in my research. It was surprising then when she suggested that we play Little Red Riding Hood.

"It's my favorite fairy tale." She smiled. "Except there are no wolves in our story, remember?"

YEARS BEFORE IT was adapted by the Grimm Brothers, "Little Red Riding Hood" made its debut in a version written by Charles Perrault in 1697. Perrault's story was adapted from the folktale, and in it he described the moment the child met the wolf, referred to as "Mister Wolf," implying that the wolf stood for a human being.

In Perrault's version, when Little Red Riding Hood arrives at her grandmother's house, the wolf is lying in bed and asks her to undress and join him. Little Red Riding Hood is alarmed to see his disrobed body and says, "Grandmother, what long arms you have," to which the wolf replies, "The better to hug you with." Perrault's version ends with the wolf devouring Little Red Riding Hood, followed by a short poem that teaches the moral of the story: that good girls should be cautious when approached by men. As for wolves, he adds, these take on many different forms, and the nice ones are the most dangerous of all, especially those who follow young girls in the streets and into their homes.

Perrault presented his readers with a somewhat refined version of the popular folktale, which was originally filled with sexual seduction, rape, and murder. His version speaks to the deceiving nature of nice wolves, who hurt their victims while pretending to offer something special, presenting sexual perversion as a form of love. It was to become even more highly refined over the years to the point where the sexual innuendo was entirely omitted and the story transformed into a children's fairy tale.

While fairy tales usually differentiate between good and bad people in ways that help children organize their world and feel safe, "nice wolves" leave children confused, unsure of what is dangerous and what is not. Abused children end up feeling that they themselves are bad, that they have done something wrong. That confusion of tongues between love and perversion will haunt them for years.

"You are Little Red Riding Hood," Lara says, and hands me the puppet of the girl with the red dress.

"She is going to visit her grandmother," she says and then whispers, "The girl thinks the grandmother is an old lady but she is actually a wolf."

"A wolf?" I repeat her words and remember how she kept stating there were to be no wolves in our story.

"You will see." She smiles as if hiding something. "You will see what I mean soon. The grandmother has a lot of secrets."

But we don't find out what the grandmother's secrets are, nor do we ever get to her house. Instead Lara instructs me, as Red Riding Hood, to sit under a tree and wait for her to come pick me up.

"I will be back soon," she says firmly.

She turns her back to me and starts playing on her own.

I am left to sit there for a long while, knowing that I have been assigned to be the girl that Lara has been, lost alone in the woods, overwhelmed by the secrets of others.

Sitting there in silence, waiting for Lara to come back, I feel like the little girl I used to be, when I was left to wait for my parents to come pick me up from the candy store. My "me-search" enters the room and I realize what I am looking for. I suddenly remember what I always knew.

I was seven years old, younger than Lara. I had started second grade in a new school far from our home. During the first week of school my parents had told me that we were planning to move to a new apartment, closer to the new school, but until then I should wait at the candy store after school and they would pick me up from there.

Every day, I walked to the candy store on the corner and waited, exactly as they'd told me to do. Moses, the owner of the store, was a kindly old man with a white mustache and a big smile. I liked him. I believed that he liked me too, and I especially liked that he gave me candy.

As a little girl, there was nothing I loved more than candy. My mother, in an attempt to feed us healthy food, did not allow it in the house. She used to serve us plates with sliced apples and dried fruit. "Candy made by nature," she called it.

When Moses offered me candy for the first time, I was thrilled and ate it as fast as I could. He looked at me and smiled. "I see that you really love it."

The following day he offered me ice cream that he kept in a freezer in the back of the store. "What kind do you like?" He had a cone in each hand. "Vanilla or chocolate?"

I pointed to the vanilla one.

"Why did I know you would choose that one?" he teased, and then asked if I wanted to come pick out something from the back of the store.

"I will let you choose whatever you like," he said.

Moses always smiled, and his kisses were ticklish and wet. Once in a while his wife would come to the store and he would put a little chair for me in the front and ignore me until she left.

When my dad arrived to pick me up, Moses would tell

him what a good girl I was and wave goodbye. "See you tomorrow."

I liked waiting for my parents there, but as time passed I started feeling nauseous.

"Moses gives you too much candy," my mother would say. "That's why your stomach hurts."

But that wasn't the reason. I wasn't sure why; I just knew that I didn't like it when he hugged me so tight. I still liked him even when I didn't.

In third grade I stopped liking Moses. We moved to our new home and I tried to avoid walking near his store. Only years later was I able to put it all together and understand what had really happened in the first few months of second grade. I never told anyone, and I wasn't always sure if it had actually happened or if I'd imagined it.

Freud viewed memory as a fluid entity that was constantly changing and being reworked over time. He referred to this dynamic as *nachträglichkeit*, translated into English as "afterwardness," which means that early traumatic events are layered with new meanings throughout life. Freud was especially focused on sexual abuse as an event that would be reworked retrospectively as the child got older and reached certain developmental phases. Sexual abuse in childhood isn't always registered by the child as traumatic. The child is overwhelmed with something they cannot process or even make sense of.

As time passes, the traumatic experience is reprocessed. In every developmental phase the child will revisit the abuse from a different angle and with different understanding. When that abused child becomes a teenager and then an adult, when they have sex for the first time or have children, when their child reaches the age they were when the abuse happened — in each moment the abuse will be reprocessed from a slightly different perspective. The process of mourning keeps changing and accrues new layers of meaning. Time will not necessarily make the memory fade; instead, the memory will appear and reappear in different forms and will be experienced simultaneously as real and unreal.

NINETEEN YEARS AFTER I first met Lara, it is a gloomy day in mid-September and I'm about to meet her again. It is also my birthday.

In the intervening years, I've had three children. I have stopped working with children and am now only seeing adults. My office is in the same neighborhood as it was nineteen years ago, in downtown Manhattan.

I open my door and look at the tall young woman who stands there. I do not recognize her.

"I grew up quite a bit." She smiles as if reading my mind. "Thank you for answering my email so quickly, and for agreeing to see me."

She sits on the couch and looks around.

"I like your new office."

I recognize her smile and these first words.

"Those were your exact words when I met you for the first time," I say, trying to learn something about her from the way she looks: the black T-shirt, the black long silk skirt, her sneakers and blue nail polish, and her long straight hair, which I think used to be curly. I'm trying to read what has happened to her in the years since then. Where has she been? Is she happy? Did she find out what really happened?

"I know it's your birthday today," she then says to my surprise.

I nod and smile. Some things don't change. She still knows more about me than I expect.

"Don't worry, I can't read your mind," she adds as if reading my mind. "When I tried to find you, I googled you, and one of the first things I found on your Wikipedia page was your birthday. I was happy you scheduled our session for today. I really wanted to give you a gift."

Traditionally, therapists do not accept gifts from patients. The contract with our patients is clear; there is no dual relationship, no exchanges other than our professional services for an hourly fee. Psychoanalyst and patient share a joint goal of trying to explore the unconscious; therefore, it's interesting to understand when and why a patient brings a gift and what that gift represents. But in reality nothing can make a gift feel unappreciated and dismissed more than analyzing it.

Lara opens her bag and hands me a small puppet. It is a girl wearing a red dress. Our Little Red Riding Hood.

She surprises me again.

"Do you remember?" she asks, and she suddenly sounds like the little girl she used to be.

"Of course I do. I never forgot," I say.

We look at each other. I like her as much as I did all those years ago, and I wonder what has made her look for me now.

"I came to see you because I need your help." She answers the question I haven't yet asked out loud.

We start where we stopped years before. Lara tells me about her family's move back then to the West Coast. It was sudden; she didn't even have a chance to say goodbye.

"In retrospect maybe we were running away," she says. "Running away from the unhappiness my family lived in. But the unhappiness followed us and in fact only got worse."

The tension between Lara's parents, Hanna and Jed, became intolerable, and four years later, they got divorced. Jed lost his job and had to move to work in Denver. Hanna grew even more depressed and was hospitalized. Lara found herself alone, and at the age of fourteen she had to move yet again, this time to live with her grandmother Masha.

Lara talks and I feel sad and worried. How was it for her to move again, to separate from both her parents? To live with her grandmother, whom she used to have mixed feelings about?

"At that point things actually got better," she continues. "My grandmother was wonderful and my life with her was so much easier. I realized why my mother loved her so much. She supported me and understood how hard this new living situation was for me. She was caring and gave me everything I needed. Once a week we traveled together to visit my mother in the hospital, and once a month we visited my father. At some point, after my mother was discharged, I made the decision to stay and live with my grandmother permanently."

I listen to Lara and remember the way Hanna used to talk about her mother, defend her, describe how in spite of the fact that she believed her mother was responsible for the break in their family, she loved her and could never fully blame her. When Jed expected Hanna to cut her mother out of their life, she refused. Now Lara expresses the same feelings about her grandmother. Something has changed since her grandmother was our bad wolf.

"My grandmother grew up in Russia with eight siblings," Lara tells me. "She is the youngest and the only one who is educated. She values education and encouraged me to go to graduate school. In fact, she'll be paying for my doctoral degree," Lara says and then smiles shyly. "I decided to study psychology. I was just accepted into a PhD program." Then she starts giggling. "Maybe I want to be you. I mean, as a child, therapy was the only time I didn't feel alone. I felt that you really wanted to know me."

Lara takes a deep breath. She looks tired and I see how hard she tries to be likable, easygoing, not depressed like her mother. She was always tuned in to others, making sure she was not a burden on them and instead taking care of those around her.

"You said you needed my help." My voice sounds softer than usual as I ask, "Tell me, what brings you here today, Lara?"

Lara stares out the window for a long time.

"Your old office used to have big windows looking at Grace Church, I remember," she says, still gazing outside. "There was a coffee place across the street and I used to sit there with my father every week after therapy. He would order fresh mint tea and a croissant, and I would get a baguette and use all the chocolate spreads that were on the table. Every week we would sit there silently, eating and not looking at each other. He never asked me how therapy was. Maybe he was too afraid to know. And I didn't think about anything else but the sweet spreads that my mother didn't like me to eat and that made the end of a session less bitter. I never liked separations.

"I remember sitting across the street, staring at the entrance of your building, hoping to see you walk out and wave to me. I didn't want you to meet anyone else after I left. I wanted you just for myself. And I wished that my father would say something, ask me something, it didn't matter what. Even one question would have been enough, so we wouldn't have to sit there in silence. I wished that he would wonder out loud if I liked the spreads and which one I liked most. I would point to the hazelnut chocolate, and maybe then I could tell him about Little Red Riding Hood's basket that we packed just before the end of the session and how I put unhealthy candy in it and nothing else. I wished that he would smile and say that he knew I loved sweets because he noticed that I ordered the spreads after therapy every time. But he didn't ask anything, and I wasn't sure that he noticed what I was eating or anything else about me."

Lara pauses and looks straight into my eyes.

"There are many questions from my childhood that were never asked. There was no grown-up who could know the answers. There is a mystery that I wasn't able to resolve on my own," she says, and I know what she is talking about.

LARA AND I start meeting again once a week. She begins her doctoral program, trying to find the topic for her dissertation, her "me-search." Her mind will lead us to the questions that were never asked. Her research question will be born in that void and so will the truth.

It is a winter day when Lara comes in holding an old picture; in it she is thirteen years old, with a backpack on her shoulders. She is wearing gym clothes and is smiling at the camera.

"This is from the time before my parents got divorced," she says, and I recognize the girl in the picture; she looks very much like the girl I knew.

"I will never forget that day; it's when I got my period for the first time. My mother took this picture and then called my grandmother to tell her that the 'aunt was visiting' or something funny like that." She pauses.

"I heard them fighting for the first time. My mother was crying and yelling at my grandmother. I couldn't hear what my grandmother was saying but I knew it was bad. I knew she made my mother very upset and I felt terrible. I thought it was all because of me.

"It was the one time I remember asking directly: 'Mom, what happened?'

"'It's nothing; it's between me and Grandma,' my mother said, but I didn't give up. 'What did she say? Why are you crying?'"

Hanna told Lara that her mother had asked her to cut Lara's hair short.

"My mother told me that and started crying again. She

thought it was the meanest thing one could do to a girl. She thought it was crazy. She told me that when she was about my age and got her period for the first time, my grandmother took her to the barber and without further explanation had her hair cut short. She remembered looking in the mirror and the tears running down her cheeks. 'I look like a boy,' she sobbed.

"'Why did she do that?' I asked, but my mother didn't answer. I asked again, 'Mom, why did Grandma do that to you when you were my age?'

"'Sometimes it's hard to understand Grandma,' my mother answered. 'She brought strange traditions from her country, from her own childhood, who knows.'"

Lara and I are silent. I wonder if she has the same thought I have. Does she realize that her grandmother was trying to protect her daughter by making her look like a boy and not a girl? Did she try to protect her daughter, and now her granddaughter, from sexual abuse?

No one wanted to know. No one ever asked.

I remain silent, asking myself if Lara is ready to question her family history.

Our wish to know everything about our parents is a myth. Children are in fact often ambivalent about learning too much about their parents. They don't want to know about their parents' sexuality and often try to avoid knowing intimate things from their history.

"I need to know what really happened," Lara says decisively and points her finger at the girl in the picture.

The girl in the picture smiles a fake smile.

"My grandmother," she says, touching her long straight hair, "was always so protective of me. She accused Ethan of abusing me, but then after my parents got divorced that was all forgotten. No one talked about it anymore. That was strange."

Lara looks severe. She suddenly seems much older than her twenty-nine years. She takes a brief glimpse at her watch, calculating how long we have until the end of the session. I know she needs time to think through her history.

"When I lived with my grandmother she used to scare me," she says. "She used to repeat that I had to be careful. She would tell me strange things, for instance, that I needed to wear underwear to bed, otherwise worms would get into my vagina. She would whisper it and I remember feeling nauseous. Every time she talked about my body she would start whispering. When it came to sex her boundaries were strange. She talked about inappropriate things as if they were normal and about normal things as if they were perverse. Her whispering made me feel dirty, as if she had dark secrets that came out at night, and then in the morning she would be my loving grandmother again."

"When you were ten years old and we played Little Red Riding Hood, you told me that the grandmother in the story had a lot of secrets," I say. "'You will see,' you used to repeat, 'you will see.' But we never found out what those secrets were. Maybe you are ready now to ask the questions that were never asked."

LARA TRAVELS TO meet with her grandmother Masha. She wants to learn about Masha's childhood and hopes to find her own answers there.

Masha grew up in a chaotic household with very few resources. Her parents went to work early in the morning and came back late at night. Her oldest sister, who was thirteen, became her main caretaker. Masha told Lara that she always felt her mother didn't want her, that deep inside, her mother regretted having so many children. Masha was a shy girl and a good student. Excelling at school was her way to feel special and worthy.

One night, when Masha was ten years old, she had a bad dream. She often had bad dreams but knew she couldn't wake her parents up or they would be upset with her. She sneaked into her fifteen-year-old brother's bed. Her brother was the smartest; he was funny and brave and the one she admired the most.

He kissed her.

From then on her brother came into her bed every few nights. She would make believe she was asleep and wouldn't make any noise. He would touch her gently and never hurt her. In the morning they behaved as if nothing had happened.

It was when Masha was about thirteen and got her period for the first time that her mother told her in a very matter-of-fact way that she shouldn't let her brother in her bed anymore.

"Do you mean her mother knew?" I can't stop myself as I interrupt Lara, who is still shaken by what she learned.

Lara nods. "Yes, but they never talked about it. She never told anyone."

Unprocessed experiences always find ways to come back to life, to reenact themselves again and again. Masha's repressed memory came to life in the typical way repressed memories do. It snuck into the mind unexpectedly, triggered by later events. For Masha, Ethan and Lara were a reminder of her and her older brother. That close relationship between a brother and a sister awakened her own repressed memory, and she felt the urge to give Lara the protection she never had, to be the parent she herself had always wanted. Her request that Lara's hair be cut short was an attempt to protect Lara, in the same way that Masha believed she protected her daughter, Hanna, when she became a woman. Through Lara, Masha relived her own sexual abuse, which she could never fully process.

Sexual abuse is one of the most confusing traumatic experiences that we know. The intergenerational aspect of sexual abuse is unique in the way that each generation overwhelms the next and inflicts on it the drama of their sexual trauma.

The next generation's world is often sexualized in the same way that the victim was sexualized as a child. They feel flooded by the parent's unintegrated sexuality and perplexing boundaries. As Lara describes, innocent, trivial things, such as the underwear she wore when she went to sleep, were filled with sexual meanings. The adult — in this case Lara's grandmother — who tries to make sense of her own feelings often communicates to the child the confusion about what is safe and what isn't. The original confusion between innocence and perversion is played out through the next generation, with seduction, promiscuity, and prohibition all intermingled. The next generation usually describes growing up with a constant, vague feeling of violation that only later in therapy is understood to be related to the original break of boundaries in their family's history of sexual abuse.

In her article "Enduring Mothers, Enduring Knowledge: On Rape and History," Dr. Judith Alpert describes how sexual abuse can present itself in the mind of the next generation. Using her own childhood experience, she discusses the way traumatic thoughts and "memories" can be transmitted from parents and grandparents and present themselves in the child's mind as their own. That phenomenon leaves everyone, the child and her caretakers, with the confusion that is at the core of sexual abuse. As in Lara's case, our challenge is to hold all generations in mind — grandmother, mother, and child — as victims of either sexual abuse or the intergenerational inheritance of sexual abuse.

Masha, who was reliving her own unprocessed trauma, devastated her family with the idea that Lara's brother sexually abused her. Lara became more and more overwhelmed. It was as if she were reliving her grandmother's repressed feelings. Through the family's ongoing rumination and the premature introduction of sex, Lara felt the intrusion into her body and thus the scene of sexual abuse was reenacted.

"When I was sitting with my grandmother last week and she told me about her childhood, I cried. She didn't," Lara says, and tears drop down her cheeks. "I tried to listen to her the way you listen to me, and to help her understand that she could tell me anything and I wouldn't judge her, that I really wanted to know her.

"At some point she stopped and said she didn't want to talk about it anymore. But she kept talking and I didn't say a word. She started blaming herself, saying it was she who went into his bed first. Then she started to question her memory and said that it all sounded much worse than it actually was, that things were different then.

"Before we went to sleep she made me a cup of tea and served it with a slice of the chocolate cake she had baked for me.

"'I know how much you like chocolate,' my grandmother said, and hugged me. Then she held my shoulders, making sure I looked at her. 'Lara, please don't take my problems on you,' she said. 'I don't want you to be sad because bad things happened to me. Worse things happen to people. That's life; my life isn't so special.'

"'You had to keep a secret for so many years, Grandma,' I said, and hugged her as tight as I could. But she just kept nodding. 'I didn't keep a secret. It was something I didn't always remember. The secret kept itself.'"

"I think I found my 'me-search,'" Lara tells me as she wipes her tears.

She will go on to study the tormenting and deceptive impact of incest and sexual abuse on the next generation, those aspects that are hard to research, as they are seemingly irrational, puzzling, and unformulated experiences, but that Lara lived through in her own childhood. We both recognize that one way to face that transmission from generation to generation is to process those experiences and help others process and own them, too. Demons tend to vanish when we turn on the lights.

3

SEX, SUICIDE, AND
THE RIDDLE OF GRIEF

"I'M CURSED," LEONARDO whispers, looking straight into my eyes. "Do you know what I mean?" He then concludes decisively, "You know what I mean. Of course you do."

Leonardo started coming to see me two years earlier, right after a breakup with his partner, Milo. In the first months, he couldn't stop crying. He said that although he knew he and Milo never got along, his pain was intolerable.

Two years have passed and his agony has not diminished. He still feels paralyzed, lost. He tells me that he is not ready to meet anyone else and fears that he will remain sad forever.

"Somehow I'm stuck," he says, and we agree that at this point it seems like his grief is not just about Milo anymore. We try to understand what it is that he lost when that relationship ended.

Separations are emotional deaths that we have to mourn. In breakups, we always lose more than just the person we love. We lose a life, a future, everything that we have dreamed about and hoped for. And while we know *whom* we have lost, we might not understand *what* we have lost.

Leonardo and I try to figure out what it is that he keeps mourning.

"I want to move on," he says. "Milo and I were together for only a year and I have been grieving for two years already," he says, irritated. "I wish you could program my brain and delete parts of my memory so I could forget my past and move forward."

I understand that the ongoing pain makes him wish he could erase the past and never look back. He feels haunted by the past. But it is not yet clear to either of us why.

"I don't love Milo anymore, and still, I feel like I have lost a part of myself, and now I'm supposed to function without it. And it hurts so much," he says. "How do people ever recover from a loss without feeling that a part of them is gone forever? Do they ever fully recover?" he asks, diving right into the riddle of grief.

Freud went back and forth in framing and reframing his thinking on loss. One of the questions he kept investigating was how much people can let go of their loved ones, or whether they always keep a part of themselves connected to the love object.

Freud's thinking was influenced by his wish to understand his own grief. He suffered painful losses, including the death of his daughter Sophie from complications of the Spanish flu and the tragic death of his beloved four-and-a-half-year-old grandson, Heinele. According to his biographers, the death of his grandson was the only occasion in Freud's life when he shed tears and described himself as depressed.

At first, Freud explained that the grief process was about letting go and breaking the tie to the one we have lost. From that perspective, a healthy process is when the drive to live is stronger than the wish to reunite with the dead (what he called "the death instinct"), and so we slowly detach and loosen our "cathexis," the energy invested in the lost person.

Later, Freud developed his thinking to differentiate between mourning and melancholia. He described that in mourning the world feels poor and empty, while in melancholia, the person herself feels poor and empty. She loses interest in the outside world, she loses the capacity to love, and her self-esteem is diminished. That melancholia, according to Freud, is an unconscious process in which, instead of detaching and withdrawing the emotional investment from the lost person, the melancholic preserves and keeps that person alive inside them through identification with the dead. If the person is me and I am them, then there is no loss. Keeping the lost person caged inside denies the loss, but at the same time it holds the melancholic person forever captive to it. As a result, she loses parts of her own investment in life and vitality.

Whereas Freud's two categories of mourning and melancholia were defined as opposites, in reality both conditions take place in different ways for different people. The process of mourning is multilayered, and a certain identification with the person we have lost, either to death or in a separation, will always take place. Like Leonardo, many people feel that they have lost a part of themselves with their loved ones. Many feel that they are dying with the dead, and they struggle with melancholic identification with those whom they have lost.

The question Freud and many after him kept trying to explore was what a healthy mourning was, and how much we can actually let go of our loved ones.

In 1929, Freud wrote in a letter to the Swiss psychiatrist and founder of existential psychoanalysis, Ludwig Binswanger:

We know that the acute sorrow we feel after such a loss will run its course, but also that we will remain inconsolable and will never find a substitute. No matter what may fill the gap, even if it be filled completely, it nevertheless remains something else. And actually, this is how it should be. It is the only way of perpetuating that love which we do not want to relinquish.

Here, Freud emphasizes that the loved one is always present, even as we slowly fill the gap of her or his absence. A part of us moves on, and another, more hidden part remains "something else," connected and loyal to that love.

Life goes on and we visit and revisit our separations and losses. We mourn them again and again, every time from a different place. We think about them, discover new layers, process from different angles. We accept them and give these losses new meanings.

The process of separation requires slowly letting go of the attachment to the other person. In many cases, what is called "melancholic grief" results from a loss that we are unable to fully comprehend and therefore to let go. Leonardo and I wonder in what way he has tried to grieve something he is still unable to fully know or identify. It is impossible to grieve an unrecognized loss, yet without the process of mourning, one's life is imprisoned by death.

"YOU KNOW HOW I always tell you that I feel cursed?" Leonardo begins the next session annoyed. "Now Milo chases me even in my dreams."

He tells me that he has dreamed about Milo again. In the dream Milo was knocking on the bathroom door, calling his name.

"I don't know what this dream even means," Leonardo says. "He knocked on that door, decisively, trying to force me to open it." Now he sounds angry. "He is trying to force me to come out."

"To come out." I repeat his words and both of us recognize the association with being gay.

"You know that in my family being gay was never a big deal. I always thought my mother was actually happy about me not bringing girls home, and my father, until his last day, was so accepting. He used to say that as long as I'm happy, that's what's important." Leonardo thinks for a moment and then adds, "I honestly think that it was because his own father committed suicide when he was a child. He just wanted me to be happy. He was afraid of sadness."

I know what he is referring to. Leonardo's grandfather had died by suicide when his father, Jim, was a child. A few days before his fortieth birthday, he had locked himself in the bathroom and hanged himself. His nine-year-old son, Jim, knocked on the door and then ran crying to his mother, who found his father after it was too late.

"For years this was our family secret," Leonardo says. "My grandmother never told people the truth. She would say that he died suddenly. If someone pushed her, she would lie and say that he had died from a heart attack that he'd had in the bathroom and drowned. They were so ashamed of it, as if it meant something terrible about us."

"What a secret to carry," I say, and Leonardo nods. "What do you think this dream means?" he asks me.

"In your dream, it is Milo who knocks on the bathroom door," I say.

Leonardo looks a bit puzzled. "Yes, he begs me to open the door, exactly the way I imagine my father, as a child, had. How strange. What do you think it is? How is my breakup from Milo related to my grandfather's suicide?"

I don't know the answer yet, but like Leonardo, I, too, recognize that in this dream his father is replaced by Milo knocking on the bathroom door. I ask him to tell me more.

"I think my father knew deep inside that his father was unhappy and didn't want to live," Leonardo says. "I'm not saying he thought he would kill himself, but the truth is that for years my father felt very guilty, as if he could have saved him. He told me that story many times; even in the last years of his life he still talked about it. Unlike my grandmother, or maybe in reaction to her hiding it, my dad refused to keep it a secret. I think I was maybe five years old when I asked him how his father died, and he told me the truth. I guess he didn't want me to grow up with secrets."

"Can you tell me that story again?" I ask. "Tell me what your dad remembered about that day your grandfather died."

"My dad told us this story so many times that I visualize it in my mind as if it is a movie I'm watching," he says. "I imagine him pounding on the door, calling his father's name, begging him to open the door. And I see him crying into his pillow at night, blaming himself for not saving his father's life: if only he had been stronger he could have broken down that door, or if only his father loved him enough he would not have left him."

Leonardo's eyes fill with tears. "It is a pretty extreme thing to do," he says, "killing yourself when you have three young children at home. I don't know. I want to feel bad for my grandfather, but then I mostly get so angry with him."

Suicide, and especially a suicide of a parent, has serious implications for the surviving family members. The immediate survivors are overwhelmed with conflicting feelings of devastation, sorrow, anger, and shame. It leaves them with so much guilt that in order to cope they project it outside. The guilt turns into blame, and the question — whose fault was it? — is often the main pathway to releasing the intolerable guilt.

Suicide is traditionally explained as a redirection toward the self of a murderous impulse originally aimed at others. That act of destruction leaves a loaded inheritance for the next generations, who will remain to hold the ghosts of suicide. They will struggle with the darkness of the soul, with buried secrets from the past, and often with their own suicidal wishes. Many of them will excessively invest in the well-being of others as a way to compensate for the unprocessed guilt. Their fantasy might be to save others in ways they couldn't save the person who killed himself.

Suicide can become a family myth, usually filled with unanswered questions.

I wonder out loud, "What is the story behind your grandfather's suicide? Why did he do it?"

"I often ask myself that question," Leonardo answers. "I'll tell you the craziest theory I have," he says, but then he pauses and falls into a long silence.

"It feels like you are holding a secret," I say.

Leonardo smiles. "I wouldn't call it a secret. It's something I used to joke about with Milo, a wild thought that I always had, that Grandfather was actually gay and that his suicide was not the real secret my family kept, but his sexuality."

Leonardo leaves and I am left with the feeling that there are layers of truths unrevealed, unspoken facts from his family history as well as a hidden identification he has with his grandfather and with what he believes led to his death. That underlying identification sent Leonardo on

an unconscious mission, which I locate in his dream —
to liberate the family from shame and from a destiny of
self-destruction.

IN THE FOLLOWING sessions, Leonardo and I dive into
his family history, trying to explore his secret identification with his grandfather: the feeling that his dead grandfather lives in him and that Leonardo needs to live out
something for him and for the whole family.

There are many unanswered questions, but I realize
that the more we talk about his grandfather's sexuality,
the less space Milo takes up in his mind. As time passes
and his symptoms of depression slowly subside, Leonardo
becomes certain that he has figured out his family secret,
and he decides it's time to find out the truth.

"I didn't want to feel that I was crazy and that I made
up all these theories about my family," he tells me one
morning, describing how, at his cousin's wedding the previous night, he decided to ask his aunt.

"My whole family was there, my two aunts, my father's
younger sisters, and their children. I really like my family
and I was happy to see them, and you know, I love wed-
dings." He smiles. "The pathos of forever and ever until
death do us part, isn't that romantic?" Leonardo is playful
and I recognize his fantasy about romance and death.

"My aunts were very close to my grandmother, and I

figured this was my chance to learn something about the years before my grandfather died and know what's only in my head and what is real. Let me tell you, the good news is that I'm not crazy. The bad news is that it's worse than I imagined.

"After the ceremony, one of my aunts came to me in tears and said how sad she was that my father hadn't lived to celebrate that day with us. She told me she was thinking about him the entire evening. That gave me an opening. I asked if she was also sad that her own father hadn't lived to see her children and grandchildren.

"'May he rest in peace,' she answered. 'I was a baby. I didn't know what it was to grow up with a father. You know, your father, my older brother, was like a father to me.'

"And then I asked her, directly, 'Why did he kill himself, do you know?' My aunt didn't hesitate. 'Leo, these were different times. There was a big drama. He couldn't live his life the way he wanted, like you.'

"I was so glad that you and I had talked about this for so long," Leonardo says to me. "Because I got it right away. I knew what she was talking about. At first it irritated me because I thought she meant gay people now are free to be who they are, which is obviously totally not true. I tried to say that, but she cut me off.

"'He had this secret and then my mother found out. She was pregnant with me when they discovered that he used to have sex with men. My mother never told me how it all came out. I only know that there was a scandal. A few months later I was born and then my father killed himself.'"

Leonardo pauses. "Can you believe that?" he asks. "My first feeling was relief. I thought, 'Thank God, I'm not crazy.' But then I thought, 'Oh my God, my poor grandfather, how awful for him,' and it made me feel angry with my aunt for saying that he used to have sex with men. What a dismissive thing to say, as if he was not a full person with feelings."

Leonardo pauses again. He doesn't look at me, and we sit in silence for a long minute before he continues.

"Now I understand why it was so important for my dad to make sure I knew that he accepted my gayness. I always felt that it was related to his father's suicide but I didn't know how. And I'll tell you something else. I think my grandfather was in love with a man and that's why he killed himself. I think he was in a relationship and that he was forced to end it. The family devalued it by making it only about sex, making it sound dirty so they could frame it as bad. But it was about his identity. It was about love and loss. Can you see that?"

Leonardo raises his head and looks at me. I notice the tears in his eyes.

"This is what my dream was about," he says. "My father's wish to save his father from a breakup that felt like death."

"From a death your grandfather couldn't fully mourn," I say.

Philosopher Judith Butler describes the idea of "grievability," the notion that some things, lives, or relationships are not considered valuable, and therefore if they were to be lost, that loss wouldn't register as such. It is only lives that were acknowledged by the culture as having a value that we consider worthy of grief. Some lives, some loves, some races, sexual orientations, and identities, are seen as less valuable or are not recognized as lives at all. Butler writes, "Grievability is a presupposition for the life that matters."

There is no way to grieve what is not considered lived. When love isn't recognized as such, it is not grievable, and one is left mystified and inconsolable.

As in Leonardo's case, the loss that couldn't be fully mourned lives in its raw form in the unconscious of the next generation. They are left to process old losses that don't fully belong to them and to mourn what originally was ungrievable.

LEONARDO AND I begin to piece together a picture of the context of his loss of Milo: his grandfather's struggle with his homosexuality and his identity; his inability to mourn the loss of his illicit love; his suicide, leaving behind a devastated little boy, Jim, who believed that if his dad had only loved him enough he wouldn't have left him.

Many layers of unprocessed loss. A known secret that shelters another secret, a forbidden one.

For years, Leonardo's father kept the gift he had made for his father for his birthday, just a few days before he died. He had created a small ceramic vase in the futile hope of making his father happy for a day and keeping him alive. Jim had clung to this vase as a child, and then for the rest of his life. When Jim died, Leonardo inherited it, and he kept it on a shelf in his clothes closet.

But it wasn't only the vase that he had inherited. It was also the trauma and the losses of earlier generations, unprocessed losses that were held in his closet and in symbolic ways lived with his own belongings, until it was too hard to differentiate what was his and what wasn't.

Leonardo picks up his bag. "Maybe I'm not cursed after all," he says as he heads to the door. "Maybe this is just a sad story with a hopeful ending."

HE WALKS INTO the next session looking pleased. "I had a good week and I even met someone," he says. "I feel encouraged."

He opens his bag. "Also, I brought something to show you." He pulls out a small box wrapped in layers of newspaper. "I had to bring it in, just to show you how amazing this is."

There it is, a small blue ceramic vase: his father's vase.

"For years," Leonardo says, "I imagined my father as a boy, holding in his hands this gift he made at school for his father's birthday in his favorite color, blue. That gift that I saw so many times as a child, and that I kept in my closet after my father's death."

Leonardo pauses and then exhales deeply in relief. "Only after our last session," he says, "did I realize what I've been using it for."

He hands me the vase and I peek inside, where I see three single, mismatched cuff links.

I look at Leonardo, puzzled.

He explains that he stored each of them there when they lost their mate.

We look at each other and Leonardo shrugs and smiles. "They've been waiting all these years for their loved ones to come back."

4

THE RADIOACTIVITY
OF TRAUMA

In Israel, Holocaust Remembrance Day, Yom Ha'Shoah, is a national holiday.

Each year, in mid-April, everyone observes two minutes of silence. By 10 a.m. all children are standing in a circle in the schoolyard waiting for the sound of the air-raid siren, signaling that the silence is to begin. Everyone pauses whatever they are doing. Pedestrians stop walking, diners in restaurants stop eating and stand up, and on the busiest highway, every single car pulls to the side and people step out to stand still. It is time to remember the six million who were murdered during the Holocaust.

As children, we learned that terrible things can happen to people. This wasn't an explicit statement but a fact that — like a hot spice added to our food — had become a regular ingredient in our lives. In almost every apartment building there was someone from "there," the Europe of World War II, a Holocaust survivor. We usually knew who those people were, even if we didn't know their history, even if we didn't see the numbers tattooed on their arms, even if we were often afraid of them, devastated by their life stories.

In the schoolyard, when the siren began, we tried not to catch each other's eyes, imitating the teachers, who kept their heads down. We tried as hard as we could to stay serious, to feel sad, to think about the concentration camps, the gas chambers, to imagine our own families being there. It was important, we learned, never to forget. But as hard as we tried, inevitably as the siren began one of the kids would start giggling, and we would cover our faces, trying not to burst into laughter.

Nervous laughter during the Holocaust Day siren is a familiar childhood memory of people who grew up in Israel, where horror stories shape part of the national identity and a special form of dark humor characterizes the younger generations.

Years later, in New York City, far from my homeland, I am surprised by how many of my patients are second- and third-generation descendants of Holocaust survivors. These high-functioning, successful, and productive people all have something in common: the ghosts of persecution who show themselves in unpredictable ways and at unexpected times. Under the surface they carry the trauma and guilt of the survivors.

I learn that from childhood, images and daydreams of the Holocaust have been frequent visitors in their minds, even and especially for those whose parents never talked about what happened to their families during the war. The memories of the Holocaust live inside them even as they are unknown to them, and those invasive thoughts and images are often trivialized. Sometimes I learn about them only years into the therapy.

When their stories are told, we recognize how that history has shaped their present lives. We identify the ways in which the past continues to play itself out in the present and how they live and relive their families' untold stories.

RACHEL'S GRANDFATHER WAS a Holocaust survivor. She mentions this briefly during our first session when I ask about her family history, but she doesn't feel it is relevant to her current life. It certainly isn't the reason she came to therapy.

"So many things have happened in my family since. So many good things. There is nothing else to say." Rachel smiles and apologizes. "Every family carries some trauma. This is our story, and it happened so long ago. How many years since the Second World War?" She looks at me and immediately answers, "More than seventy, I think.

A long time. My grandparents have already passed away," she says.

Rachel's grandfather was born in Budapest and he survived Auschwitz. When the Second World War ended, he immigrated to America, where he met Rachel's grandmother, who came from a Jewish family that had escaped Europe when the war started. They fell in love, and a year later Rachel's mother, their only child, was born. Her grandfather never talked about what happened during the war, and her mother described her childhood as a normal suburban American one.

On the surface their family trauma ended when her grandfather left Europe and left the past behind. Rachel came to therapy to talk about other issues, to discuss her ambivalence about having children, a topic that was a source of tension with her husband, Marc.

I am always curious to understand my patients' life choices — why they choose to have, or not to have, sex, relationships, a family, a career. As the narrative unfolds, the gaps between what people want to have and what they can tolerate having become apparent. Why do so many people want love but can't find it? Want a career but can't succeed? Want to move forward but get caught in the same cycle over and over again?

It is not unusual for people not to be able to handle or tolerate having what they think they want. Beneath the urge to have or not to have is usually another layer that navigates our lives. There is an unseen, unconscious part of us that might go against our conscious goals and even attack and undermine them. In fact, everything we don't consciously know about ourselves has the power to control and run our lives, in the same way that the riptides below the surface of the ocean are its most powerful forces.

We are especially conflicted when it comes to change. Behind the wish to make money, have a career, or have children, we might locate resistance to change, a hidden ambivalence about growing up, and a struggle with separation and loss. We might want a romantic relationship but at the same time resist or reject it, often because we need to protect ourselves from being vulnerable, abandoned, out of control, or consumed. Some are unconsciously loyal to their original families (particularly if they perceive that family as superior to other families), which makes it hard for them to belong to anyone else. Others feel emotionally responsible for one of their parents and therefore anxious about separating and leaving them. They maintain their childhood structure and worry about changing their position, being loyal to their family myths and legacies.

A change is a slight goodbye to our past: to our child-hood, to our familiar roles, to our known selves. To develop, to create, is to separate and live the future as opposed to cherishing the past. An unprocessed past will not allow us to move forward. It will hold us as the gatekeepers of our history.

The search for her truths brings Rachel to question her dilemmas. She wants to know who she really is and what the hidden forces are that run her life. We wonder which parts of her feelings about having a child are authentic and which are defensive. When it comes to the topic of having children, we therapists need to be very careful not to confuse social norms with psychological goals. Our aim is to free people to make decisions. The freedom to choose is a therapeutic achievement.

"Why would I want to bring a child into this world?" Rachel answers a question I didn't ask and thus advances a profound dilemma that we fully understand only later.

At this point, the argument about whether or not to have a child seems to exist solely between Rachel and her husband. Marc thinks they should have a child and she feels uncertain, confused, ambivalent. But quickly Rachel's internal conflict shows itself, and it becomes clear that both the positive and the negative voices belong to her and that she is arguing with herself. To have or not to have?

Rachel talks about her fears. "This world is a terrible place to bring babies into," she says. Her voice becomes loud. "Seriously, what can I promise a child? A world of wars? A planet that will be destroyed? Racism, hate, and violence? What will my children promise *their* children? It's just so selfish to think that this universe needs more children when so many of them live in misery."

She tells me about her plan to leave New York and move to a different country. She thinks maybe she and Marc will be happier somewhere else.

"Where would you like to move?" I ask.

"To Israel," she immediately answers. I must look surprised, because she adds, "I know you are originally from there. It's not because of you that I want to move there. I always wanted to live in Israel, since I was a young girl. I'm not sure why."

Rachel tells me that the homeland I have left behind is the promised land of her fantasy.

"If I had a child, I would like to live there. Did you know that every young child in Israel learns about the Holocaust?" she asks.

There is a moment of silence. I remember the schoolyard and how we all stood there waiting for the siren. I remember the Holocaust survivor who visited our class when I was in second grade. She told us about her childhood, that when she was our age she walked barefoot in the snow for hours, a story that we referenced every time someone complained that they were cold.

"You would never survive the Holocaust," we would tease one another.

I remember that in fifth grade, during recess, the kids made a list of all the places where people hid from the Nazis. We discussed where we could hide, and I thought of the stories of mothers trying to quiet their babies so they wouldn't expose the hiding places. That night I couldn't sleep. I imagined my baby brother crying as the Nazis came to our apartment. The next day, I decided to practice hiding with him. I packed his pacifier and some baby toys, and I took him with me into our bedroom's closet. We stayed there for what seemed like a long time. Every time I heard a noise, I shushed him, making sure he didn't expose our whereabouts. When I heard my mother coming, we got out and I put him back in his crib. It was a secret that only many years later, when my brother was a grown-up, I shared with him.

The Nazis were always in our nightmares, and as children we were afraid that the bad guys would find and kill us.

"Yes, every child in Israel knows about the Holocaust," I say to Rachel. "Do you wish you had known about it when you were a child?"

"Yes. I really do. As a child I heard about it but I didn't learn about people's lives and their personal survival stories. I didn't see the photos, like those I saw years later of kids in striped uniforms. I just knew that something bad had happened to my family in Europe."

Rachel's family tried to protect the children from their own trauma and therefore never talked about it. Rachel was left with the knowledge that something terrible had happened but she didn't know what exactly. She had a bad feeling that she couldn't put into words. Rachel wishes there were a family story she could tell, or a concrete picture that would help her know what was real and what was only in her imagination.

An important question comes to the surface. Is it better for the next generation of trauma survivors — the inheritors — to know, or not to know? Does it even matter, assuming our ancestors' trauma finds its way into our minds anyway?

This dilemma preoccupies many parents, who worry about the impact of their suffering on their children and try to minimize the damage. Parents want to protect their children from carrying their pain, and children try to protect their parents from having to reveal and relive their traumas. The unconscious collusion between parent and child is one that aims to avoid pain, and it contributes to the repression of those experiences, which become unspoken secrets.

Descriptions of traumatic events are overwhelming and might create a "secondary trauma," an emotional distress that happens when we are exposed to another person's trauma. Disturbing reports or images inflict cruelty: they reenact the traumatic event and traumatize those who didn't directly experience it.

In Israel after World War II, survivors didn't talk about the Holocaust. Being a survivor was a source of shame, and it was only years later that talking about the Holocaust became normalized and an inherent part of the culture. However, being exposed to the horrors of the Holocaust from such a young age doesn't only educate but often also traumatizes Israeli kids. Without fully knowing it, they live and relive the history of the Holocaust.

Remembering and reenacting suffering is part of the Jewish tradition, and it is threaded through many rituals, such as the Passover seder, where the "memory" of slavery and liberation is relived through our senses and our actions. The reenactment of trauma links the past and the future, our history and our destiny. It turns passive victims into active agents, victims into victors.

The identity of the Israeli state, founded only three years after the Holocaust, is based on the ongoing Jewish trauma of persecution and on the dream of creating a safe home for the Jews. It is that dynamic of turning passive into active, which I discuss at length in Chapter 7, that aims to liberate victims from defeat and helplessness while denying their own aggression.

The dilemma of memorializing of trauma on the one hand holds the need to honor the victims, to cherish an identity and a legacy, and to try to prevent crimes from happening again. On the other hand it binds together past, present, and future as one. The next generation is called to identify with the previous one, and it will be entangled with the trauma and losses of those who came before.

When it comes to talking about trauma, we always walk the delicate line between too much and not enough, between what is too explicit and what is secretive, what is traumatizing and what is repressed and thus remains in its raw, wordless form. We are usually caught in that binary between the two extremes because when it comes to trauma, regulation is always a challenge.

Rachel tells me that she wishes she knew more. Her family story was silenced and her unprocessed family trauma became a repressed secret with no words or symbolic thinking associated with it. Those kinds of secrets live as strangers within our minds, ones that we can't identify, touch, or change, that are passed to the next generation as phantoms, felt but not recognized.

"As a little girl, I used to be afraid of everything," Rachel says. She pauses for a long while.

"You know, when I was six years old I started sleeping with a knife under my pillow," she says softly. "My parents didn't know about it. It was my secret. I remember the first time I did this. It was midnight and everyone was already asleep. I went to the kitchen. I looked in the drawer, found an orange knife, and took it to my room."

"What were you afraid of?" I ask.

"That night I'd woken up from a scary dream. In my dream I'd been holding a baby, and someone was chasing us. I was supposed to protect that baby, and I ran with it in my arms." She looks at me and adds, "I remember this well because after that night I had that dream almost every night, for many years."

"Did you hide with the baby?" I ask, remembering hiding with my baby brother.

"No, I couldn't find a place to hide, so I just ran and ran. There was no shelter, no place I could feel safe."

I imagine Rachel running for her life, a baby in her arms. She was just a child when she started to have this recurring dream. As we talk, many questions come up: Who is that baby? Is it Rachel herself, who feels unsafe in the world? What and whom was she running from?

There was nowhere to hide and babies were not safe in that world.

I ask her to share any associations that came to mind when telling me the dream.

"The Nazis." She nods. "It's the only thing that comes to mind. Maybe I'm in Budapest, running from the Nazis. I slept with the orange knife every night. In the mornings, I would hide it in my desk, then I'd put it under my pillow again before I went to sleep. I never told anyone about it until now."

"You felt unsafe then and you are afraid to bring a baby into this unsafe world now. You don't want the baby to feel the way you did as a child," I say.

"I want my child to be able to tell me anything. And if she or he is afraid, I want to hold the baby tight and help it feel safe."

Rachel starts imagining her own child. The more she talks about her childhood fears, the more she realizes why she couldn't bear the idea of having a baby, assuming it would experience life the way she did. Not having that baby is her way of protecting it.

Rachel sighs. "I had to hide my panic. I couldn't tell anyone about it. I didn't want them to think that something was wrong with me. My fear was the biggest secret of my childhood," she says.

For years Rachel felt as though she carried a forbidden secret, but perhaps, I wonder out loud, her secret was a way to keep the secrets of others.

"What was your grandfather's secret?" I ask.

Rachel doesn't answer. She looks at me seriously.

"Who knows," she whispers.

A FEW MONTHS later Rachel gets pregnant. She gives birth to a baby girl, whom she and her husband name Ruth.

I'm excited when she comes to my office with Ruth, a tiny baby with a sweet face. Ruth looks at me and smiles.

"Of course you are smiling." Rachel holds her baby and speaks in a gentle tone. "You remember her voice from when you were in my belly." She points at me. "Yes, you know that she helped your mommy have you. She made me realize that I can create a bubble of safety for you in my arms."

Rachel puts Ruth on her chest and Ruth falls asleep. She tells me that her mother chose the baby's name. She told Rachel and Marc that this was the name she had wanted to give Rachel when she was born, a name that was written on the candle her parents used to light every Holocaust Day, but her parents strongly objected to that idea.

"Ruth was a family member who was murdered at Auschwitz," Rachel explains to me. "So when my mother wanted to give me that name, my grandparents argued that it was a bad idea. 'There is no need to burden a baby with the name of one who died,' my grandmother said to my parents with tears in her eyes. She looked at my grandfather, who stood there silently. My mother told me that her parents used to say that Jewish babies are the most important evidence that the Nazis didn't win, that they didn't destroy us. 'Here is our next generation, right here,' my grandmother said. 'She should have an optimistic name.'"

Rachel's mother tried to convince her parents, but the more she argued, the more upset they became, and at some point Rachel's grandfather got very angry.

"A new baby should be connected to the future, not to old worlds. Our granddaughter should be associated with happiness, not with horror. What is wrong with you?" he shouted at Rachel's mother, and left the room.

"This was the most emotional my mother had ever seen him, before or after," Rachel tells me. "He was a pretty steady, rational guy. She almost never saw him cry. She told me that when she was sad as a little girl, her father would pick her up and hug her until she could hardly breathe. Then he would look at her and ask, 'Are you feeling better now?' And when she nodded, he would set her back down and, without looking at each other, they would each go to their rooms. They never talked about emotions, and my mother didn't know anything about his past. She only knew that he came from 'there' and that his whole family had been murdered at Auschwitz. She didn't know how he had managed to be the only one who survived, and none of us dared to ask."

The past, Rachel and I now realize, was required to be forgotten. After that fight, her parents gave up. They named their baby Rachel. In the Bible, Rachel was the love of Jacob's life, and Rachel's parents knew she would be the love of theirs.

Rachel's grandparents died when she was young. Years later, when her mother suggested the name Ruth for their newborn, Rachel and Marc immediately loved it.

"I want my baby to be connected to our family history. I want her to know who we are," Rachel tells me. "I researched and found that Ruth was a popular name in Hungary in the 1930s. I'm sure my grandparents didn't want to be reminded of that, but as the next generation, I want not only to face the past but also to cherish it." Her face lightens as she looks at Ruth, who is sound asleep.

At this point Rachel and Marc begin exploring the possibility of moving with Ruth to Israel.

"I'm going to fulfill my childhood dream," Rachel tells me with a smile. "I feel so lucky that Marc can get a job there. Did I tell you that he has family there? I grew up with very few relatives around. My grandmother was an only child; she had an aunt who she was not in touch with. And there was no one on my father's side. But in Jerusalem we had one family friend, a man who had survived the Holocaust with my grandfather and who was like a brother to him. After the war my grandfather immigrated to America, and his friend went to Israel. We used to visit him during the summers, and I remember his daughter and his granddaughter, who was more or less my age. I'm sure he has died by now, but I wonder if his family is still in Jerusalem."

Rachel opens her phone and swipes through her pictures. She finds one from her childhood album and hands me the phone. It is a photograph of Rachel at the age of eight with another girl; they are holding hands and smiling for the camera.

"This is in the old city market of Jerusalem," she explains. "I don't even remember the girl's name. We are planning to visit this spring, to work out the details of moving there. Maybe I should look for this family. It would be really special if I could find the granddaughter, don't you think?"

A FEW MONTHS before their planned visit, Rachel wakes up covered with sweat. From that night forward, she starts having sleep terrors. Right after she falls asleep, she suddenly jumps out of bed, screaming in fear. She is confused, worried about what is happening to her.

Sleep terrors are caused by the overarousal of the central nervous system, and research shows that the majority of people with post-traumatic stress disorder (PTSD) suffer from those terrors. Unlike nightmares, which are bad dreams with story lines, sleep terrors usually involve a strong feeling of fright without a clear narrative or story attached to that feeling. The person wakes up screaming and doesn't have a dream to report. Because people don't usually remember these events in the morning, it is not surprising that historically, sleep terrors have been attributed to demon possession or other ghostly activities.

Rachel is upset. As in her childhood, at night she feels that she is in danger, that she is about to die. Something frightening is happening that she can't explain. Her symptoms are clearly connected to emotional material that she doesn't have access to. We assume this is related to her upcoming trip.

As we begin exploring the nature of her night terrors, they begin to change, and a familiar nightmare reappears instead.

"I'm running for my life, a baby in my arms. It is exactly the same dream I had when I was six, the dream that made me put the knife under my pillow." Rachel looks confused and frustrated. "I stopped having that dream maybe fifteen years ago. Last night I was back there again, only now I have a real baby at home, and the baby in my dream looked like Ruth. It is so upsetting," she cries in frustration.

The trauma that no one in her family talked about has invaded her mind.

Professor Yolanda Gampel of Tel Aviv University identified what she calls "the radioactivity of trauma," a metaphor borrowed from the domain of nuclear physics. It describes the monstrous and destructive effects caused by sociopolitical and horrifying violence. We cannot be protected from the impact of events that took place many years ago and in places far away, even when we didn't experience them ourselves or don't know their details. Like a nuclear fallout, the emotional and physical radiation of disaster spreads into the lives of the generations that follow. It shows itself in the form of emotional and physical symptoms, a reminiscence of trauma, of an attack on one's life.

The traces of the past are everywhere. Repressed secrets become nameless dread. They live in our psyche, like radiation, with no form, color, or smell. The mind cannot prevent the psychological invasion of destructive aspects of the past, and in Rachel's case, her family trauma plays itself out over and over again.

"I don't know anything about what happened then," Rachel says. We look at each other and she adds, "My grandfather mentioned once that they arrived at Auschwitz on a beautiful spring day. The place looked green and peaceful but one thing bothered him: a strange, overwhelming smell, kind of sweet and unfamiliar. In retrospect, the scent of death."

We are both silent.

"My grandfather was a young man when the war started. He lost all his relatives. He was the only survivor."

"Who did he lose?" I ask.

"I have no idea." Rachel sounds frustrated. "He talked about the weather at Auschwitz. He talked about his best friend, who survived with him. But he never told us about the family he lost.

"I want to know who Ruth was," she adds, and there is a new spark in her eyes. "I understand that my nightmares are being triggered by this trip, but I think I should not cancel it. I should look for my grandfather's friend's family and find out. I owe this to myself and to all of us."

Rachel had planned the trip for mid-April, without realizing she was going to be there for Holocaust Remembrance Day. She was going to look for traces of her family history and try to put a narrative to the disturbing images she has carried inside her since she was a child.

NAMES ARE A significant part of one's identity. In first sessions, I usually ask people about the meaning of their names, inquire who chose the names for them and why, and wonder if there are specific meanings or stories associated with their names. Names are connected to emotions, the hopes parents have for their child, who they think the child will become or want the child to become. A name reflects the parents' feelings about having that child. It contains remembrances from the past as well as a vision of the future.

Babies are often named after relatives or others who passed away. A child might be given the name of a person the parents loved, admired, or attributed certain characteristics to. The child's name might reflect certain expectations, responsibilities, or roles. For example, one of my patients was named after his mother's father, who died just before my patient was born. In therapy we connected his name to the role he was assigned at birth, as his mother's caretaker. His mother described him as a mature and responsible baby, wise from a young age, whom she turned to for advice. Another patient was given a name by his mother that meant "mine." It turned out that his father was ambivalent about having a child; she felt this baby was hers alone.

As I describe in Part II, there is a profound meaning in naming a baby after a person who died in tragic circumstances, for example, a child or a person who died by suicide or was murdered. Doing so is often an expression of a wish not only to revive what was lost but also to repair the past and heal trauma.

In mid-April Rachel, Marc, and baby Ruth go to Israel — to look for their future, to search for the past, to find out who Ruth was. What they discover is unbelievable but in fact also quite believable. Suddenly everything makes sense.

In Jerusalem, Rachel, Marc, and Ruth meet the family of her grandfather's friend from Auschwitz. His friend had died years earlier, but the man's daughter and granddaughter are happy to see them. They invite them to the daughter's house in Jerusalem.

"We met them on a Sunday morning," Rachel tells me. "I had never felt such a breeze as on that day in Jerusalem. We walked into our hosts' home, with Ruth sleeping in the sling, and were invited to sit on the porch. As we sat down, Ruth woke up, and I introduced her to the family. 'This is Ruth,' I said, and the daughter looked at me, startled. She didn't say a word and went to the kitchen to bring tea and cookies. When she came back, she said, 'How meaningful that you named her Ruth. My father used to talk about Ruth. He said that your grandfather never recovered from her death. That a part of him died with her.'

"I didn't know what to say. I was too embarrassed to tell her that I had no idea who Ruth was. That I only knew from my mother that she was a relative who had died at Auschwitz and that her name was on the memorial candle my grandparents used to light every holiday. I couldn't breathe and instead kept silent. Marc looked at me and knew what I needed. He turned to our host and asked if she could tell us everything she knew about Ruth.

"And then we discovered my grandparents' secret. She told us that when the war started, my grandfather was married and had a daughter named Ruth. She was still a baby when they arrived at Auschwitz. His wife and daughter were separated from him and taken to the women's section. He never saw them again. Someone told him they were taken to the gas chambers and murdered just a few hours after they'd arrived."

Rachel tells me that while they were talking, a siren sounded. Their hostess apologized for not preparing them. "What a symbolic moment," she said. "Today is Holocaust Day. The tradition is to stand in silence in memory of the six million who were murdered."

They all stood for a long moment until the siren ended. Then the granddaughter said, "I'm sure that was strange for you; it is never easy for us either." Her voice was tender. "I work as a teacher, and kids here tend to giggle during the siren. I remember this from my own childhood. Coming from a different country you probably understand that it's a lot for children to handle, that it's hard for them to process the horror."

Rachel looks at me and starts to cry.

We feel the ground shift, realizing that this secret nightmare has been her way to live the memory of an unimaginable trauma. As the narrative of the past takes shape, we watch Rachel's ghost turn into an ancestor. She finally has a story that she can tell rather than relive again and again.

The room is quiet but for the muffled sounds of her tears and breath, less labored now.

PART II

OUR PARENTS

The Secrets of Others

THIS SECTION UNCOVERS our parents' secrets and hidden realities from the times before we were born and from our infancy. It explores known as well as unknown losses of siblings and the impact those have on the surviving children and on their offspring. It describes the enigmas of unwelcome babies — children of unwanted pregnancies and their constant struggle to stay alive. It looks into the eyes of fathers and fatherhood and further discusses the relationship between reparation and repetition: our wish to heal our parents' trauma, to cure their wounded souls, which instead can lead us to reliving and repeating their painful histories.

111

It is the ability to accept that which cannot be changed or fixed that allows us to start mourning. That permission to grieve for our losses and faults, as well as for our parents', connects us with life and welcomes the birth of new possibilities.

5

WHEN SECRETS
BECOME GHOSTS

My patient Noah has been preoccupied with death for as long as he can recall. When he was eight years old, he read the obituary section of the newspaper daily. "I wonder who this person was," he would say, as he tried to share his interest with his mother. But she would shrug. "You can never really know."

Noah wanted to know; he needed to know. He was searching, investigating. Who had these dead people been? Whom had they left behind? How old were they when they died? Could Noah die? Could his parents?

Decades later, Noah comes to see me with what he calls his "obsession with dead people." He wants to know everything about these people in the obituaries, and I want to know everything about him. With each obituary that

Noah brings into the consulting room, we piece together our respective puzzles, hunting for what is missing.

"I got it," Noah reports after hours of painstaking research at home, googling, filling in dates and details of the latest obituary. "I think I know everything. Now I can let it go."

Unlike Noah, I don't get it. Missing many parts of Noah's personal history, I try to wait patiently for them to enter the room. I know from experience that sooner or later the missing pieces will appear. I just have to silently listen and invite them in.

Noah becomes irritated when he is missing something in his puzzle. He holds the newspaper and reads aloud to me from the obituary of a woman named Marie, then rolls his eyes. "Listen to how annoying this is," he says. "How come they write that 'Ronald' was her second husband? If you google him, you find this same Ronald was also the translator of a book she co-authored many years earlier with her first husband — who was also named Ronald."

I am confused and jokingly think, Maybe she only liked people named Ronald. My reaction is a result of the fact that I have trouble following the details, which makes me anxious. I don't yet fully understand Noah's interest in these facts about the dead.

"Both of her husbands were called Ronald — is that possible?" Noah wonders. He counts the Ronalds again, as if he needs to make it clear that there is something behind those names.

He holds in his mind those who have died, and he refuses to let them go. He embraces their stories as if they belong to him, and in that sense those people are neither alive nor dead but rather exist as ghosts between two worlds, never fully seen but present in his life, and now in mine as well.

As I join Noah on his search, I become aware that ghosts — the ghosts of the dead, the ghosts of his history — haunt us both. We always know less than we want to.

"How old was your mother when you were born?" I ask him one day, trying to imagine his family.

Noah answers: "Forty-four, I think. Old, right?"

He is almost forty-four and doesn't have children of his own.

"Are you old?" I ask.

"I guess so," he says. "Growing up as an only child to parents in their mid-forties wasn't easy, and for some reason, I always imagined I had a twin brother who died at birth. My mother used to get annoyed when I joked about it. She thought it was another of my crazy ideas about death. I secretly imagined we were both Noah. Noah One and Noah Two — like Thing One and Thing Two from the Dr. Seuss story."

"And you, are you Noah One or Noah Two?" I ask.

"Of course I am Noah Two; do I look like a Noah One?" he replies playfully and adds, "It reminds me of Ronald One and Ronald Two from Marie's life. Do you think she loved them equally? Don't you think she married Ronald Two only because she missed her first Ronald and wished he were alive?"

I listen to Noah and think about the lonely little boy that he once was, preoccupied with the idea of the death of his parents and what he calls his "bizarre fantasies" about a lost brother. There are so many gaps in his narrative, and in therapy we try to fill them in: to imagine who he used to be; to consider the meanings of his dreams and fantasies; to understand his childhood yearning for a brother and the anguish he constantly felt but couldn't quite name.

As time passes, Noah stops investigating obituaries and begins to talk more about his own psychic losses, his symbolic deaths. We talk about the imagined dead brother as representing the "dead" parts of himself, including his depressive withdrawal from the world, and the emotionally deadened aspects of his parents, both of whom are still involved in his life. His mother, especially, has always struck him as disconnected, as if she is emotionally invested in something she has left behind.

One Saturday night, I receive an email from Noah. "Dr. Atlas," he writes. "This morning, two shocking things happened. I couldn't wait until our session to tell you." The first is that his mother died early that morning. The second is that he has found his dead brother.

"This morning," his email continues, "as I hugged my father, he told me that there was one thing they never wanted to burden me with. He said, 'We decided when you were little that you would never find out the secret until one of us died.'" The secret is that there was another son, about a year older, who died before Noah was born. His name was Noah.

"My parents have reserved their burial plots next to a very small grave," Noah goes on. "We will bury my mother there tomorrow afternoon. Noah One was buried there forty-four years ago, at the age of eight months, just a few months before I was born and named after him. They did not want to weigh me down with that, to cause me pain or devastation."

After decades of searching, Noah Two can now complete the obituary.

As surprising as Noah's discovery seemed to me at the time, when I published his story in the Couch section of the *New York Times* in April 2015, neither of us expected the response it got. In the hours after the column was published I started receiving emails from people who wanted to share similar experiences.

What Noah believed was his own esoteric story turned

out to be the story of many people, each of whom in turn had assumed it was a cryptic and unusual thing that had happened only to them. People shared their stories of lost siblings, secrets they only uncovered later in life, and the ways those secrets showed themselves in their minds. Several wrote about discovering they had a twin who had died at birth and the impact of that trauma on their lives. Those coincidences between the secret reality and the way it appeared in their minds were often experienced as seemingly irrational, and sometimes hard to believe. All of these people were left with a powerful link between their past and their present, between a feeling that they initially couldn't explain and family trauma. Most didn't know how to make sense of the strange synchronicity between those family secrets and the way their minds and bodies responded to information they didn't consciously know.

I heard from a man I'll call Benjamin, who said that for years, since he was a little boy, he had a dream in which he was buried underground. He would wake up frightened in the middle of the night and he would tell his parents that he was afraid to go back to sleep because he couldn't breathe. His parents hoped that this dream would fade as he grew up but in fact things got worse, and at the age of thirteen Benjamin developed claustrophobia. His panic would be especially severe when he needed to take the subway. No one understood why he had developed these fears.

Benjamin always knew that his mother's family had been murdered in the Holocaust. He knew that she didn't have her parents, grandparents, or uncles; that she had immigrated to the United States as a little girl survivor; and that she had met his father when she was sixteen years old. It was only when Benjamin was in his forties that he learned about the way his grandfather had died — he had been buried alive. His parents, unaware of the features of their emotional inheritance, had never made the connection between his nightmares and other symptoms and their family's traumatic history. As in Rachel's story in Chapter 4, as horrifying as it was, learning about his grandfather's brutal death allowed Benjamin to stop experiencing and carrying that fact in his body. When our minds remember, our bodies are free to forget.

I also heard from Amy. Her story involved nightmares, too, and a memory that was processed through the body. One day in her early twenties Amy woke up from a horrible nightmare. In her dream, she had been on an airplane that crashed, and she was burning alive. Amy hadn't known her father. He had died in an airplane crash when her mother was pregnant with her, and Amy grew up with the fact of his tragic death but never thought it had affected her life. Why was it that she had suddenly experienced his trauma as if it were her own? Why, in her dream, was she the one who was burning to death? The nightmare recurred, and for a month Amy couldn't go to sleep without feeling that she was about to die. She started to have panic attacks, and the traumatic image of the burning plane didn't leave her. She went to see a doctor and to her surprise found out that she was pregnant.

It was Amy's pregnancy that brought her family trauma to the surface: the trauma of her father who had died while expecting a baby, the trauma of a pregnant woman who had lost her husband, and the trauma of an unborn baby who would never meet her father. Her body knew what her mind couldn't remember.

The idea that people are connected to one another beyond the conscious mind and communicate with one another in nonverbal ways has always been a topic of psychological investigation. Unlike in popular culture, psychologists do not attribute those aspects of our minds to magical thinking or to supernatural phenomena, but to a basic concept: the unconscious.

Unconscious communication is the idea that one person can communicate with another without passing through consciousness and without intention or even awareness on either person's part. The implications of this are profound — we are interconnected in ways we don't fully recognize and cannot control, and we know more about one another than we are consciously aware of.

Amy lost that pregnancy and for the first time got in

touch with the grief she carried underneath: mourning a baby never born, a father never met. As it had with Noah, unprocessed family tragedy kept Amy unconsciously connected to the past, identified with the dead, whom she had never known. Unburying their family traumas, processing the losses and the profound impact those losses had on their lives, allowed each of them to untie their invisible bond to the past and free themselves to create their own future.

6

UNWELCOME BABIES

JON DOESN'T REMEMBER his sister, Jane. She died when he was only a few months old. Throughout his childhood, he heard stories about her tragic death. He knew that she had been riding her bike in the suburban neighborhood where they grew up, on her way to visit a friend, when she was hit by a car. She died right away. Jane was twelve, the oldest and the only girl in a family of five children.

Each of Jon's three older brothers has his own recollection of that morning in mid-May. His middle brother remembers the dress their mother was wearing. His third brother says he can't forget the sound of the siren, but he isn't sure if it was from the ambulance or the police car that came to inform them of Jane's death. His oldest brother, Jake, swears that his mother dropped the baby, Jon himself, as she was running out the door, but their father insisted that had never happened.

They all feel that their parents were never the same after Jane's death.

As if bound by an unspoken agreement, the family members avoided talking about Jane. They knew that mentioning her name might cause their mother to blame them for something.

"Why did you leave the cabinet open?" she would say angrily. "How many times have I told you to not eat with your mouth open?"

The brothers all remember the day they asked their father to buy them bikes and how their father tried to convince their mother that it might be a good idea.

"Especially because of what happened," he said. "The boys shouldn't be afraid of riding bikes. All the experts will tell you that it's the right thing to do," he argued with their mom.

That same evening, their mother packed a bag and announced that she was leaving. She told them she was planning to throw herself under a train. Jon remembers the boys chasing her, screaming and sobbing.

"Mommy, please don't leave."

They ran after her to the street, and the farther she walked the louder was their weeping.

They never asked for bikes again.

Every year, in May, the family went to visit Jane's grave. They would stand there for a few minutes, the boys observing their parents washing the gravestone, and then they all left in silence.

Jon remembers the bad feeling in his body, the pain in his stomach, and a sense that he had done something wrong. But he never understood why he felt that way.

At the age of thirty-five, Jon had what he described as a nervous breakdown.

Six months later, he decided to start therapy.

On the first day we meet, he says of his breakdown, "It came out of nowhere. One day I was okay and the next I fell apart."

I ask him to tell me about his life before the breakdown. I want to know more about who he is.

Jon tells me that he married Bella a few years ago and that they have a little girl.

"Her name is Jenny," he says and pauses for a long moment. "I had a sister who died when I was a few months old. Her name was Jane." He continues, "When my daughter was born, I wanted to cherish the memory of my sister, but I didn't want to name her after my sister. I was afraid my sister's name might bring her bad luck or maybe, God forbid, it would impact her life in other bad ways. You know, some people say that it's not a good idea."

Jon looks embarrassed. "I hear how I sound," he says. "Bella and I decided to choose a name that starts with the letter *J*."

I realize that his own name starts with the letter *J.* I hear his conflict about his daughter's name: on the one hand, the fear of hurting Jenny, and on the other, his unconscious wish to bring a part of his sister, Jane, back to life.

I ask him to tell me about his sister.

Jon seems hesitant. "I don't remember anything," he says. "I mean, I was just a baby so it's not my memories that I'm telling you but things I heard from other people. I just know that my siblings experienced a real trauma. They knew her; I didn't. So it didn't impact me as much."

"It was hard for everyone but not so much for you, is that what you mean?" I ask.

I see him thinking.

"A different kind of hard, I guess," he answers. "Everyone around me was obviously sad. Sad is not even the right word. They were broken.

"And me, I don't know what my story was, to tell you the truth. I was just left alone. To my own devices, as they say." Jon smiles and adds, "I don't even have a story of 'this and that happened to me,' except for what I already told you. That's it. Honestly, I have almost no childhood pictures. My brother Jake told me about my mother dropping me on the floor when she heard about my sister's accident, but that probably didn't even happen. I don't want to make things up." He looks troubled. "People tell me that in therapy you can build a whole story about your child-hood. Not that I mind doing that, but a story about what? It's like having empirical research without any data; it can't work; that's all I'm saying."

Jon is worried about making up a false life story. Instead, he builds a narrative filled with emptiness. He doesn't seem to appear as a character in his own childhood, and I'm left wondering about his ability to take part in life. It's as if Jon wants to make sure he doesn't fully exist.

While most people have some childhood stories and memories, it is not unusual for people not to know much about their early life, especially about the time of their birth and early infancy. We don't always know if our parents planned the pregnancy or if it was an "accident." In fact we don't always know who our biological parents are. Postpartum depression and other crises from the time we were conceived or from our early life are often covered up with romantic myths. When things go wrong, secrets are born.

While the first year of a baby's life has an enormous impact on their future, exploring a patient's infancy is especially delicate, as we rely on the narratives of others and on what they let themselves tell, know, or even remember.

The secrets of infancy are unformed events that leave traces in our minds but have no narrative attached to them. They are, therefore, the skeletons of our existence.

They remain hidden inside us even as they give shape to our forms.

Jon and I begin with the present moment and with the little that we know: he has a baby daughter, and trauma happened in his family when he was a baby. His sister, Jane, and his baby, Jenny, are connected in ways that we don't yet fully understand. His childhood is clouded by his sister's death. He never stopped to think about the past and instead marched forward, as far as possible away from his history. Until the day he fell apart.

Jon takes me all the way back to the beginning of his life, and I'm aware that those journeys are usually the most puzzling of all.

After he leaves my office, I realize he has left a pacifier on his chair.

A week passes and I meet Jon again.

"I felt good after our session," he says. "I told Bella, my wife, that I was relieved you didn't ask me about my breakdown. I'm ashamed that I fell apart the way I did, especially given the timing, right after we had a baby and when I needed to be strong. I wanted to be as strong as my father, who, even after my sister died, was the steady one. And here I am, instead of being a man, behaving like my mom. Or, even worse, I'm not an adult but a baby who falls apart. I felt so much shame and self-hate for that. So I guess I was happy that you let me talk about the beginning of my life instead of the . . ."

Jon pauses. He looks troubled.

"Instead of the end of your life? Is that what you were about to say?" I ask.

"It feels that way," he answers softly, not looking at me.

"It feels like the end of your life," I repeat his statement.

"Yes, since Jenny was born I've been thinking about death," he says.

I realize that the beginning of Jenny's life might feel like the end of Jon's life, in the same way that the beginning of his life was the end of his sister Jane's life.

"When one is born, the other dies," I say, almost whispering, and Jon raises his head to look at me.

"That's how it feels." He nods. "But it's wrong, I know. There should be enough room for everyone."

I feel a wave of sadness. Is it possible that in Jon's mind only one of them could stay alive? Does he believe that Jane died because he was born? Is this the hidden narrative of his family?

"I'm here, in therapy, because I feel guilty," he says. "And I'm devastated by the idea that my daughter is now having the same experience that I had as a child. I'm worried that like me, she now has a sad parent who can't function. I don't want to be like my mother."

I'm curious to hear more about his mother. I imagine her sadness, her guilt, her emotional withdrawal.

Jon tells me that his mother died about five years ago and that his father died a year after that.

"Both of my parents have died, and now I have no one to ask about my childhood."

"Do you have any memories at all?" I ask.

Jon hesitates. He thinks for a long moment, then says, "I remember the porch of our house. I remember the entrance. I would come home from school and it was dark and I couldn't tell if anyone was home. I never liked that house."

"There are no people in this memory, did you notice?" I ask.

"We were four boys but I mostly grew up alone," he answers. "My brothers were older, and they left home one after the other. I left home relatively late, when I was in my mid-twenties. It's like I felt responsible for my parents and had to stay with them. And then, when my mother got sick I took care of her. I remember the last few days of her life, when she was in the hospital. It felt like she was waiting for death. I would sit next to her bed for hours, and it was the first time I heard her talking about Jane. It sounded like she couldn't wait to reunite with her."

"What did she say to you?" I ask.

"It wasn't me she was talking to," Jon clarifies. "I sat there but she ignored me and kept talking, maybe to herself, or maybe to Jane. I'm not sure, but it was okay," he says nonchalantly, "I didn't mind that Mom ignored me."

There is something touching about the way he describes himself sitting next to his mother and listening to her talking. I feel his love, his longing, his loneliness, as well as his acceptance of being invisible. He is the one who is there, but it's as if he doesn't exist, as if he is the dead child, and his dead sister is the one who is still alive inside his mother.

We sit in silence for a long minute and I realize that in my silence I might become Jon's neglectful mother, of whom he asks nothing.

Very often and without awareness, the therapist joins the patient's childhood scenario, taking the role of one of their caretakers. Childhood attachments shape the therapeutic relationship in the same way that they form other relationships outside therapy. Those who expect to be loved often make sure others love them, while those who expect to be neglected might evoke neglect. Our goal as therapists is to examine those patterns; to ask ourselves in what ways our patients relive their early relationships with us, to question who we become to them, and to process those old attachments while creating new, different ones.

As with his mother, Jon doesn't ask me for much. He shrugs his shoulders and says, "I have a baby now, and I know how hard it is. Since Jenny was born, I constantly think about my parents. They had five kids. One of them died, can you imagine? They had to take care of three young children and a baby in the aftermath of her death. No one can do that," he concludes. "Mom was broken. So yes. She ignored me."

Jon isn't angry with his mother simply because, even after she died, he still longs for her. The more neglectful she was, the more his need and longing for her increased. As a child, he had no other source of security. He tried to see her as "good" because he preferred to have a neglectful mother than no mother at all. I realize that it is easier for him to identify with his mother and with her loss than to imagine himself as a child and recognize his own pain. Unconsciously, however, he keeps repeating the pattern of neglect: fighting his unsatisfied needs and worrying about all the other ways the world might reject him.

Jon searches the room. Suddenly he points at my desk and says, "I think I forgot Jenny's pacifier here last week."

"Yes," I say as I look at my desk and recall placing it there so I would remember to give it back to him.

Jon seems unsatisfied with my one-word answer, as if he was expecting a different one. It is the first time I see him a little disappointed.

"Tell me more," I respond to the expression on his face.

"Don't you think there was a reason that I forgot it here? There must be a reason, right?" I see that he invites me to look deeper, to search for more.

"What do you think the reason is?" I ask.

Jon smiles. "That I'm a baby?" I smile back and he continues. "I feel like such a baby. Maybe what I wanted was to forget the pacifier here and go home like a grown-up."

"That makes sense," I say. "But is it possible that you wanted to both forget and also remember?"

He is intrigued, and I continue. "Maybe you wanted to forget the baby part of yourself here, but also to come back in order to dig and discover it. Maybe you want those lost parts to be found, to uncover your own life story."

Jon nods. "And what if it's not so interesting?"

I pause. I hear how afraid he is to remember how uninteresting and rejected he felt as a child. He doesn't want to feel the injury of his childhood and to get in touch with how much he needed his mother.

I think about the word "pacifier," recognizing that as a child Jon tried to pacify himself rather than cry for his mother. As an adult, he presents as an easygoing guy who doesn't need anyone to take care of him or even understand him. He doesn't get upset or express feelings of frustration, but instead tries to manage his feelings on his own and push down any emotions. Jon feels that he shouldn't depend on anyone. In his sessions, he makes sure to not feel too dependent on me, too.

Donald Winnicott, a British pediatrician and psycho-analyst, wrote that one of the most meaningful maternal functions is "emotional holding." He related that function, in parents of any sex, to the significance of the physical aspect of holding a baby. Emotional holding is the steady emotional arms and available presence of the parents that allow the baby to feel safe and protected. The parent holds the baby in his or her mind, available to tolerate the baby's emotions, tuned in to her signals. When a baby feels safe both physically and emotionally, she develops a sense of a safe world, where she can rely on the parent and trust that her needs will be met. But when emotional holding collapses, the baby usually stops turning to others and instead turns inward. When the baby feels dropped she might experience what Winnicott called "falling forever." It is the feeling of emotional collapse, an endless downfall with no bottom.

Jon learned not to reach out to his parents for soothing and to hold himself emotionally. I sense that he protected himself by giving up on his parents' comforting and re-sponsiveness. He became a boy and later on a man who didn't ask for much. He was able to manage his feelings until one day it all broke and he fell apart.

Jon leaves my office, and I am aware that we haven't

yet talked about his breakdown. I notice that he has left the pacifier on the armchair again and wonder if he keeps leaving it behind because he is the one who feels forgotten and dropped. Is he worried about me not remembering him when he is gone?

JON ARRIVES AT the next session thirty minutes early. He rings the bell while I'm still in a session with another patient.

I buzz him in, wondering if he is confused about the time for our session.

I find myself worrying about him. I picture him sitting there, in my waiting room, speculating about why I haven't let him in. I'm afraid that he will conclude that I have forgotten about him, and I imagine him trying hard not to feel hurt or angry at me.

When I finally open the door, I see Jon sitting on the edge of the chair, playing on his cell phone.

"Hey." He looks at me. "Did you expect me? I didn't mean to surprise you."

He slowly walks into my office and sits in the armchair.

"Were you worried that maybe I forgot about our session?" I ask.

"No," he answers immediately. "I just thought maybe I came at the wrong time. Maybe you were not ready for me yet. Did we say 11:15 or 11:45? I guess 11:45, right? I hope I didn't intrude. I mean, you were with someone else."

Jon moves uncomfortably on his chair and then adds, "It's not a big deal. I just thought maybe I should leave and come another time." His eyes fill with tears. "Embarrassing," he whispers.

"You thought that I wasn't expecting you. That you were rushing to come here but I totally forgot about you," I say and think about him using the word "expect" and its relation to pregnancy. I find myself wondering if his birth was planned, if his parents wanted to have another baby.

"Don't worry, it's fine," he says, both to me and to himself. "You don't have to look forward to seeing me. You are my therapist, not my mother," he adds firmly, making sure both of us know that he remembers that.

"But maybe you feel hurt because in that moment I do become like your mother, a woman who doesn't expect you, whom you think might reject you or prefer to be with someone else."

Jon looks serious. "That's possible," he says. "You know, right before I had that breakdown, I used to have those kind of thoughts and it was crazy.

"At night, before I went to sleep, I used to ruminate, thinking that my boss wanted to fire me and hire someone else. I told Bella that I had a bad feeling, a feeling that he didn't want me. In retrospect that wasn't true but for some reason I was sure that he was planning to drop me."

"To drop you." I repeat his words and point out that this is a reminder of the only story he heard about his childhood.

"You thought that your boss wanted to get rid of you, or was maybe planning to drop you, like your mother did," I note.

Jon looks at me, fascinated.

"I see what you mean," he says. "It's like I repeated the feeling that I'm not wanted, even now, with you."

I nod and Jon continues, "I swear to you, I was such a hard worker. I was the first one to come to the office in the mornings and the last one to leave at night. I thought I was a good employee but then I started to feel that they didn't like me and were planning to get rid of me. It all started right after Jenny was born." He pauses and I see him thinking, making connections.

"What do you have in mind?" I ask.

Jon looks sad. He explains to me how important it was for him to feel appreciated by his boss but that as time passed, he felt more and more rejected and frightened.

"I woke up every morning scared, feeling that I wanted to die. It was awful, but it became even worse on that morning, when something really traumatic happened."

Jon takes a deep breath. He looks hesitant, as if not sure he is able to keep talking.

"Can I tell you what happened?" he asks, and I am aware that it's not me he is referring this question to, but, again, himself. He doesn't wait for my answer.

"I had just arrived at the office when my phone rang. It was Bella. I heard her crying.

"'I need you to come home,' she said, weeping. 'It's Jenny. She fell and I don't know what to do.'

"I left everything and started running home. Like a maniac. I ran and ran, I don't even know for how long. My head was spinning with a million thoughts. I thought, 'Here it comes. She is going to die.' I thought, 'Why did I let that happen? What an idiot I am.'" He looks at me. "Don't ask me why, I have no idea. I don't know why I felt like it was all my fault. But I kept running. I heard the siren of an ambulance behind me and I panicked and tried to run even faster, to get there before the ambulance. When I finally got home I found Mom on the floor, Jenny alive in her arms."

I hear him referring to Bella as Mom, but I don't interrupt him.

"She was sobbing: 'I got so, so scared. I didn't know what to do. Jenny fell from the high chair and she didn't move. She didn't even cry. I thought she had died.'

"I looked at Jenny. She seemed okay but I couldn't calm myself down. I sat on the floor next to Bella and felt my body shaking. It's like I lost control of it and I cried and cried and couldn't stop. From that moment on, I stopped functioning. I couldn't get out of bed. I cried all day. I considered killing myself."

Jon pauses. He looks at me and repeats, "I felt that it was all my fault. The voice in my head said that I should be the one dying, not her."

There is so much guilt in being the one who stays alive. I think about Jon's sister, Jane, and about his wish to bring her back to life in his daughter, and this time, to kill himself instead. Jenny's fall was traumatic because it represented both his sister's accident and also his own childhood trauma of being emotionally and physically dropped, of being the one who stays alive but unconsciously believing that the accidents were his fault, then and now.

Jon experiences the feelings he couldn't put into words, process, or even remember: the tragedy of the baby who stayed alive, the baby who fell apart. His breakdown isn't only about his sister's death; it is, in fact, the ongoing experience of disconnection between the baby he used to be and his mother. The feeling Jon grew up with — but that he never let himself know — was the profound injury of maternal rejection. His unconscious anxiety was that she had dropped him because she didn't want him. That is the reality that was too devastating for Jon to let himself know. His solution was to please his mother and to make sure that he would disappear from his own life. Jon struggled to engage in life, constantly confronting suicidal thoughts and feeling conflicted about his right to have anything. It was through his daughter's accident that the trauma-tized child within him was awakened. He had to get in touch with his deadened self to be able to start the process of living.

Jon and I understand that the experience of his early childhood reappeared in his breakdown, and we are deter-mined to go back to that time to find out what that early experience felt like, to live through it so Jon can rejoin the world.

WEEKS PASS AND Jon feels a little stronger. We meet every Tuesday at 11:45, and he now arrives exactly on time, sometimes a minute or two late, but never early. He makes sure I am the one who is waiting for him, and not the other way around.

When I open the door, Jon walks in and always makes the same joke, "Hey, did you expect me?" he says. We both know that he is referring to the anxiety that knocking on my door might evoke in him, the worry that I won't re-member the session, that I have forgotten about him or maybe even hoped that he wouldn't show up.

But that is never the case. In fact, I look forward to seeing Jon. I'm aware of how protective of him I feel, imagining him as a baby in light of what I know about his past and about the effect of the early interactions between parents and infants on the child's later life.

At the Hampstead Nurseries in London, during the Second World War, Anna Freud was the first-known researcher to initiate careful and systematic observation of infants and children. But only much later did a revolution in understanding infants' minds begin. In the 1980s, the psychiatrist and psychoanalyst Daniel N. Stern brought contemporary infancy research into psychoanalysis and changed many old assumptions about child development. One of the most important corrections he made was to the mainstream theory from the 1960s that babies initially have an "autistic mind" and are therefore unable to interact with the world around them. Current infant research overturns this assumption; in fact, babies communicate with others right from birth. They are aware of their surroundings; are responsive to gazes, vocalizations, pauses, and facial expressions from the people around them; and engage in a constant dialogue with others.

Interactions between babies and their parents are the focus of current infant research. Video microanalysis is one method used to study and code their moment-by-moment communications. In her laboratory, researcher Beatrice

Beebe and her team at Columbia University invite the parent to play with the infant as they do at home. Using two cameras — one filming the baby, who is placed in an infant seat opposite the mother, and the other focused on the mother's face and upper torso — they generate a split-screen view of both parent and infant.

The research focuses on a few aspects of the verbal and nonverbal interactions, such as their gaze toward and away from each other (parents typically look at their infants while the infants cycle between looking and looking away, which allows them to regulate the intensity of arousal created by the eye contact). It detects their facial expressions, as well as their vocalizations, and analyzes how coordinated their facial expressions and movements are. The researchers listen to and code the vocal back-and-forth communication and the turn taking between parent and infant in that exchange.

Watching the split screen, Beebe points out that caregivers tend to tune in to the infants' movements, gestures, gazes, and expressions, and that the babies are responsive to every nuance of the mothers' behavior. There is a rhythm co-created between the infants and their caretakers. The parent usually looks happy when her infant smiles and appears concerned when the infant cries. She reduces the intensity of her behavior when the baby turns its head away; she lowers her voice when the infant seems distressed; and she tries to excite the baby when it looks back to her. The parent talks to her baby and then gives the baby a turn. The baby responds vocally in her own way. They each follow the other's rhythm of taking a turn.

Ideal exchange between parents and their infants doesn't mean absolute synchronization or "perfect" matching and superhigh responsiveness. Rather, a dynamic communication evolves that includes moments of mismatch and potential misunderstanding, followed by moments of re-attunement and repair.

These studies highlight the fact that ruptures are an inevitable part of every relationship. In fact, in 1989 Jeffrey F. Cohn and Edward Z. Tronick indicated that imperfect interaction and mismatching of communication are the rule rather than the exception. They show that a "good enough" parent is slightly mismatched and desynchronized with their infant 70 percent of the time and in synch with them only 30 percent of the time. They suggest that a good relationship is the result not of a perfect level of attunement, but rather of successful repairs. The moments when the parent re-attunes to the baby are important. They are the foundation for future trust, where both parent and infant learn that they can go back to a rhythm that allows them to be seen and understood by the other.

More than five decades of research highlight the implications of the early baby-parent interaction for future development, attachment, and mental health. Those studies predicted some of the difficulties that infants would experience later in life as children and as adults, based on the very early attachment to their caretakers. For example, a large body of research focuses on parental responsiveness, which is one of the key qualities for secure attachment. Research indicates that low maternal responsiveness at three and nine months predicts insecure attachment at twelve months, negative feelings and aggressive behavior at three years, and other behavioral problems from age ten on.

I try to picture Jon as a baby, recognizing his withdrawal as an adult. I try to imagine what he saw in his mother's eyes: her pain, her anger, her guilt, and her lack of responsiveness toward him. I wonder what he sensed even when it wasn't directly communicated to him. I am aware that there is much I don't know and may never know. Some of those early experiences are forever sealed.

JON WALKS INTO the room and sits on the armchair.

"Last night I had a conversation with Jake, my oldest brother," he says. "I told him about my therapy. I told him that a lot of things from my childhood are coming up now, especially from the time I was a baby. It was surprising, I have to tell you. I never thought I would be able to talk to him about these things, and I was shocked when he told me that he has been in therapy for years now. 'We had a lot to deal with, as kids,' Jake said, 'especially you.'

"'Why me?' I was kind of confused. 'You guys knew Jane, I didn't.'"

Jon pauses and looks at me.

"My brother Jake said that in his therapy he realized that there are two kinds of people: those who have lost and those who never had anything to begin with. 'I struggle wi h that idea,' he said, 'and I always tell my therapist that you, Jon, unlike the rest of us, who had lost, you never had. I tell her, "This is why he is the most wounded one of us all."'

"You can imagine how confused that made me," Jon says. "I told him, 'Jake, I'm not sure what you are saying.' And then he basically told me that he was eight years old when my parents found out Mom was pregnant with me, and that she was very upset and angry. She didn't want another baby, and she blamed my dad for that pregnancy and wanted to get an abortion. There were a lot of fights and they didn't talk for a while.

"'Then you were born and a few months later Jane died,' Jake said, and I felt a kick in my stomach. Everything you and I talked about suddenly made sense. They didn't want me to begin with." He looks straight into my eyes. "My parents never wanted a fifth child. Four was enough for them. They ended up with four after all. But not with the four they wanted."

We are both silent.

I'm stunned but not surprised. It is often easy to recognize those people who were not fully invited into this world. They seem like visitors, outsiders who might leave at any minute. Like Jon, many such patients don't have a coherent existence, and therefore in therapy it is harder for them to create a clear narrative of their early life.

In a seminal 1929 paper titled "The Unwelcome Child and His Death-Instinct," the Hungarian psychoanalyst Sándor Ferenczi described people who came into the world as what he called "unwelcome guests of the family." Ferenczi made the direct link between being an unwelcome baby and having an unconscious wish to die. He portrayed those patients of his as pessimistic, skeptical, filled with mistrust of others, and having suicidal fantasies. He found that they shared a common history: they were all babies of unwanted pregnancies, whether this was known to them or kept as a family secret. Ferenczi describes them as people who die easily and willingly.

Jon takes a deep breath. "I'm okay," he says. "Isn't it funny? The worst was confirmed for me, but instead of feeling bad, I'm feeling better. You know how you always used to say that I'm a baby without a story? So now I have one. Maybe it's not a happy story, but it's true, and it's mine."

I know that Jon still has a lot to process. Many questions to ask, much to mourn, to be angry about, and to forgive.

These days, when Jon walks into my office he no longer asks if I am expecting him. The mother, his mother, the one who didn't expect him, is no longer hidden and so we can now talk about her instead of reliving his relationship with her. Jon loves his mother, but now he is free to feel the insult and humiliation of rejection and of never actually having had her.

The freedom to think and to feel even the most disturbing thoughts and painful emotions brings with it the experience of being alive. It is the birthright — previously denied — that allows Jon finally to be able to choose life.

7

PERMISSION TO CRY

As a young woman I was familiar with the army unit that my patient Ben had served in; some of my friends had been in the same elite commando brigade within the Israel Defense Forces. Ben was a fighter in that unit around the same time I served in the Israeli army as a singer in the entertainment unit. In my New York City office now, thirty years later, I gather information about him and ask about his military service. He tells me the name of his unit and I write it down and nod.

I remember the day my band was sent to perform on the base of that unit. Nothing about it felt unusual or dramatic, except that I was in love with the drummer of the band and was happy that it was too dangerous for us to drive back home that night, and that we had to stay and sleep there, in Khan Yunis, Gaza. It was 1989 and I remember that we were given guns and told they were in case of emergency. I didn't remember how to use the gun although I had been in basic training just a few months earlier. My best friend and I had agreed that killing someone was bad karma, so during training we just made believe we had listened but ended up having little idea how to use the gun. On our way to Khan Yunis, it didn't feel like a big deal. In case of emergency, we thought, we would manage.

The special-unit soldiers sent us an armored bus, and a motorcade accompanied us as we drove into Gaza. The roads were bumpy and at some point the musical producer of the band, an older man in his thirties who was a musician and served in the unit as a reserve soldier, decided to sit on the floor of the bus. We looked at him, amused, and asked, "Hey, what's going on? Is everything okay?"

To our surprise, he started to cry. "My wife is pregnant. They didn't tell me we were going into Gaza. I didn't sign up for that. This is crazy."

We all looked at one another and didn't know what to do. We didn't understand why he thought it was so crazy. We had traveled to every war zone and never thought any of it was especially intense. This was the world we were raised in. In some ways, the unstable national security and our mandatory army service felt like an irrelevant disruption, and life was about the future, not the present moment or the past. It was made up of hopes and big dreams, pushing against our external reality with deep friendships, with love, and with music.

I turned around and smiled at the drummer, and he smiled back. We had our little secret and the war around us seemed like background noise.

That day, we performed in a small room, surrounded by a group of soldiers who were our age but looked older and who we believed were much braver than we were. We knew that at the end of the concert we couldn't ask them about the details of their activity or their special operations, but the truth was that we were not so curious anyway. We were more interested to hear about their high school experiences, to learn about their girlfriends at home and count the days until our army service would be over.

Now, in Ben's first session, he tells me that as an eighteen-year-old soldier he had no idea what he had signed up for, and that only now does he realize how crazy it all was.

"Most of my friends from the unit are pretty fucked up," Ben says, "but I don't have any PTSD or anything. I'm fine."

I guess we are all fine, I think to myself. A part of me truly believes that, while another part knows that it cannot be true. We are fine, but we are also not fine at all.

Coming from a culture that normalizes the experiences

that all young Israeli men and women go through, Ben talks about his early childhood in Israel and his life now in New York City. He tells me that he is married to Karen, a woman he has been with since he was eighteen, and that they are trying to get pregnant. He looks me straight in the eye and says, "Since I was a child I wanted to become a father. I'm here, in therapy, because I want to be a good father."

It is Monday morning when Ben walks into my office, a big smile on his face.

"Doctor," he says and then pauses.

When he calls me "Doctor," treating my degree as a nickname, I know he is in a good mood.

"Karen is pregnant." He smiles, then corrects himself. "We are pregnant. You know how long I have been dreaming about this baby, how hard it was for us to get pregnant." He pauses and looks at me. "I'm going to have a baby boy, I'm telling you, Doctor, I'm going to have a son." He puts his hands on his chest and takes a deep breath. "God willing, I will have a son," he says seriously.

In the next session Ben tells me about a dream: He is a baby, sleeping on his father's chest. His father kisses his cheek and whispers in his ear, "Cry, baby, it's time to cry."

"How strange," Ben says. "Parents don't usually ask their babies to cry. And fathers, they especially don't encourage their boys to be babies and cry."

"What comes to mind when you think about your father and crying?" I ask.

"That he knows I need to cry. He gives me permission, I think." Ben is quiet for a long minute before he continues. "I have never seen my father cry. Even when his own father died, even when I went to the army and all the parents stood near the buses and shed tears, my father didn't. He just walked back and forth and then he came and gave me a strong hug and said, 'No need to cry, boy. You do exactly what you have to do and may God be with you.'"

"When you were eighteen years old, becoming a man, your father told you not to cry, and now, right after you found out that you are about to become a father, he holds you in your dream and tells you that it's time to cry."

Ben nods and we realize that there is a lot for us to understand about these permissible tears, about fathers, sons, and the intermingling of vulnerability and masculinity.

Ben tells me about his father, who was born in Iraq and escaped with his family to Israel in the 1950s. Having parents who fled to Israel from Iran and Syria around the same time as Ben's father, I am familiar with the complexities of that immigration. Israel of the early 1950s was a new country. It was built on the trauma of the Holocaust.

At the end of World War II, many Holocaust survivors found homes in Israel, where they joined the Eastern

European immigrants who had left their families in Europe and moved there before the war. The immigrants who had moved before the war were Zionists and were considered "real Sabras" (or Tzabarim in Hebrew), named after the prickly pear, which has a thick skin and spikes on the outside but is soft and sweet on the inside. This term started to be used in the 1930s to differentiate the old European Jew from the new Zionist one. The Sabras were thought to be tough, physically active, and shameless, the opposite of the old stereotypical Jews, who were considered soft and passive. The new Jews were not religious and didn't study Torah; instead they were devoted to working the land, and they learned how to fight, first in the resistance movement and then in the Israeli army.

After the Holocaust and mostly as a reaction to it, the Israeli state was founded and became the home for Jews from all over the world. The first wave of immigrants were traumatized survivors who had lost everything in Europe. The next immigration, in the fifties, was from the Middle Eastern countries: Morocco, Yemen, Iran, Iraq, Egypt, Syria, and Tunisia, among others.

Over the years, the new country of Israel consistently privileged native-born members over the more recently arrived immigrants. The goal was to create a new culture, and immigrants were encouraged to abandon their original identity and adopt the identity of the Sabra Jew. From a psychological perspective, we can see how this was a way to cope with the massive trauma of persecution. The new Jew, a fighter, represented a transformation from a passive victim into an active victor, from a weak minority into a strong nation.

My parents, as well as Ben's parents, were part of the 1950s wave of Sephardic Jewish immigration. They came from a different culture; they spoke Arabic and were considered uneducated and even primitive. The traumatized white European hegemony discriminated against those immigrants and treated them as an inferior minority group. They lived in poverty and carried a great deal of shame not only in response to their lack of resources and their difficulty in adapting to the new culture, but also in being considered ill-mannered and culturally vile. They spoke the "wrong" language, listened to the "wrong" music, and brought with them a non-European culture and practices that were unacceptable and even threatening to the Zionist white privileged authority.

In order to become assimilated into Israeli culture, all immigrants had to speak Hebrew; Yiddish and Arabic were not acceptable. The Sephardic immigrants were asked to change their names to Israeli names, which were often given by the clerk at the border. My mother Suzan was now Shoshi, my aunt Monira was now Hanna, and Tune became Mazal. This tradition carried on for many years. Even in the 1990s, Ethiopian Jews who immigrated to Israel were asked to change their names. It was a way to communicate to the immigrants that their previous identity was unwelcome and should be replaced by a new one. It was a promise of belonging, that abandoning the past would provide a new and a better future. In reality the immigrants belonged to neither the old nor the new world; they were trapped in a cultural limbo.

My own family's immigration, like Ben's, always hovered over my childhood. I knew that both my parents had escaped to Israel as young children with their families. My mother used to tell us kids about that night in 1951 when they left Damascus. My mother was only four years old at the time. Her parents paid a Syrian man who owned a carriage to pick up them and their five young children in the middle of the night, hide them in the back of the wagon, and get them across the border.

The man arrived at 2 a.m. They all silently rushed into the back of the wagon and started riding toward the border. About thirty minutes later, to their dismay, they noticed that my four-year-old mother was missing. They had forgotten her at home. They rushed back to find her asleep in her bed, picked her up, and started the ride to the border again.

They arrived safely in Israel and settled in Haifa, a northern city on the Mediterranean Sea where Arabs and

Jews lived together. They rented a one-bedroom apartment, where my mother and her siblings grew up.

Ben's father had moved to Israel with his family from Baghdad, Iraq, when he was ten years old. During the first few years they lived in what was called a ma'abara, a refugee camp that the government had built for new immigrants from Arab and Muslim countries. In the early 1950s there were more than 130,000 Iraqi refugees in those camps. The ma'abarot were a symbol of the discrimination against Sephardic Jews, as housing policies were weighted in favor of people of Ashkenazi European descent. Camps sometimes had only two faucets for a thousand people. The toilets had no roofs and were infested with fleas, and the ceilings often leaked when it rained.

"Some people think my family was lucky," Ben tells me, "because my grandfather found a job as the cleaning person in a local school, and they were able to move to Ramat Gan, a neighborhood on the periphery of Tel Aviv. They lived in poverty. You can imagine how bad a man felt, especially from that generation, when he couldn't provide for his family."

Ben looks at me, searching for my understanding. After all, I'm not a man; do I know what he is talking about? Do I realize how painful it is to be a vulnerable man who has lost his power? I understand that Ben is telling me something about himself too, about his own vulnerability and tears and about the need to cover these in order to preserve not only his masculine identity but also his father's and his grandfather's pride.

"It was humiliating for my grandfather, the head of the family, to become an immigrant with no language, no job, no status. It's heartbreaking to think about my proud grandfather being so weak and powerless. In fact, he was never able to recover. He died with his shame, a shame about being inferior, having no respect, about speaking only Arabic, the wrong language."

At the end of each session Ben sends me a YouTube video of an Arabic song. He loves Farid El Atrash, Umm Kulthum, Fairuz, and Abdel Halim Hafez.

"My parents never felt comfortable speaking Arabic," he says. "They didn't want to feel like immigrants. But I remember the music in my grandparents' house, and my grandfather singing and shedding a tear. I used to look at him crying and knew that this music was filled with emotions, and I knew that it reminded him of the home he had left behind."

"Thank you for today, Doctor," Ben writes in an email after a session. This time he shares a link to Moshe Eliyahu and his Syrian band.

I am grateful for the songs Ben shares with me. He doesn't know that, like him, I am pretty familiar with that music; that Moshe Eliyahu was my mother's uncle, a famous singer in Syria.

My grandparents spoke and wrote in Arabic and listened to Arabic music at home. When we visited them in Haifa, it was clear that the Arabic music bothered my mother, and she used to whisper in Arabic, "Can you please lower it a little?"

Years later, I learned that at my parents' wedding, my mother's uncle, the singer, was invited to the stage. He had agreed to honor the bride and the groom and dedicate one of his famous songs to them, "Simcha Gedola Halaila" ("A Big Celebration Tonight"). My mother was devastated. The last thing she wanted at her wedding was Arabic music, and she started sobbing. Her uncle was asked to stop his singing and leave the stage. He never spoke with her again.

Arabic music became the soundtrack of my sessions with Ben. We listened to it together, and I listened to the songs Ben emailed me after the sessions, knowing that he needed to give me not only the narrative of his family's life, but also the flavors, the smells, the feelings that words alone could not convey.

Ben carried his family history, the ghosts of immigration from east to west. The Arabic music was one way to rework that history, to confront it, to turn the passive experience of being a victim of racist contempt into an active practice of celebration, pride, and ownership.

Ben, the boy who was holding his family's shame of speaking the wrong language, tells me about becoming a proud soldier in an elite Israeli commando brigade unit, where fluency in Arabic was an advantage. His was a counterterrorism unit; they performed undercover operations in urban Arab territories and often disguised themselves while speaking Arabic, gathering intelligence.

We began to process the significance of his military service and the part it played in the interplay of victims and victors, the ways in which one who feels inferior needs to become superior in an attempt to heal a trauma.

That dynamic was true on the national level as well; a country founded on the trauma of persecution raised generations of soldiers and fighters. Every war was an opportunity to repeat and repair the Jews' past defeats and humiliations. In 1982, right before the Lebanon War, the prime minister of Israel, Menachem Begin, explained why that war was necessary. "Believe me," he told his cabinet, "the alternative is Treblinka and we have decided that there will *not be* another Treblinka."

The wish to repair, and this time to emerge from battles victorious, is based on the illusion that when we do so, we become winners. But in fact a soldier's victory is never just a triumph. It's also a loss and an injury, as well as a repetition of the early trauma it was supposed to heal.

The psychological need to work through old injuries brings us back to the original scene, where we hope to transform the passive into the active, where we try to do it all over again, this time differently. We wish to relive and this time do it better, do it right, to heal ourselves through the act of reparation. Too often the attempt at reparation instead ends as merely a repetition. In our need to heal old trauma we in fact retraumatize ourselves.

The wish to heal the intergenerational trauma of immigration through becoming a commando soldier allowed Ben to feel like a victor, but it also created a new trauma that we begin to unpack, exploring the ties between fathers and sons.

As CHILDREN, THE world around us was the only world we knew and military conflicts were our reality. Kids grew up knowing that right after graduating high school they would have to serve in the army, preparing for that by trying to remember that if they stayed strong the Holocaust would never happen again.

The next step after high school was in some ways a break from life as we knew it, an alternate reality with its own rules, hierarchies, and struggles, but one we had spent our whole lives expecting. We were all soldiers and even that didn't seem strange. After all, we thought, what else would we be at eighteen?

Every year, a small group was chosen to serve in the special units. They had to go through a long acceptance process that started a year earlier, with many months of interviews, and physical and emotional tests.

Ben was accepted to serve in the commando unit.

"I was so proud," Ben says. "I didn't really think about the service itself. Acceptance was my goal. You want to be accepted, to know that out of all people, you are the one who got in." He looks amused, as if he sounds ridiculous, then adds with a smile, "Doctor, don't you think that the closest thing to it, here in the United States, is being accepted to an Ivy League college?"

I remember how proud we were of our friends who were accepted to special units. Sometimes we were surprised that those we thought of as especially masculine or brave were not accepted, and we looked differently at those who got in, as if we discovered something we didn't know about them, a secret power.

My version of being a "special-unit girl" was when Matti Caspi, a well-respected musician, accepted me into the army band that he was putting together, and my friends were proud of me. We were teenagers, preoccupied with how we looked and with what others thought of us. Special-unit boys were our omnipotent superheroes, the most desirable men, and our society worshiped them. I knew that this was Ben's victory, that he felt recognized and had compensated for his family's "inferiority" with his new sense of superiority, of pride.

We lived in the midst of the paradox of going to war and being in love with love. Love was everywhere and we lived an intensity that only the combination of hormones and war could produce. We held each other tight because we didn't know what tomorrow would bring. It was now or never.

I remember those nights when we performed for hundreds of soldiers who had not been home for weeks. I was too young to understand what I felt, that tension in the air, an energy that I don't think I've ever experienced before or since.

It was the time we performed for the Golani Brigade unit that I remember most vividly. We were invited to perform on their last day of training. The musical group performed every day and we usually didn't know in advance who our audience would be. The production unit took care of the practicalities. We just met every day at noon. Duchan, our military driver, waited for us to load the musical and sound equipment on the bus, and we drove, to the south, to the north, or to the east. We didn't really care where and we didn't mind his wild driving, thinking that if we had an accident we would finally get a chance to skip that evening's show.

The Golani base was all the way in the north, about three hours' drive from our base. We were tired and took naps on the bus. When we got there, it was almost evening and we had only two hours to put the stage together, eat something, and start the show. We looked around. The place seemed empty.

"Where is everyone?" we asked.

"They have to finish something and will come to your concert right after," someone answered.

I remember thinking, They can come whenever they want, or come late, or not come at all.

I helped the drummer put his drum set together and then checked the microphones.

"The soldiers are really looking forward to it," someone else said.

"We are too," we lied.

It was our second year performing the same show every night. At that point we didn't even like one another anymore, and we could sing those songs in our sleep. But we felt it was not appropriate to complain. After all, we went home almost every night.

"Can you play the songs faster today?" we asked the drummer. "It's already late and the soldiers are not here yet. We won't get home till late tonight."

Sometimes, when we played songs we didn't like, the drummer actually did play them faster and we all thought it was funny. But that evening was different — for some reason it felt too important.

I'm not sure where the soldiers came from, but hundreds suddenly started walking toward us. All of them were wearing their olive uniforms, as were we, but theirs looked dusty, and each soldier was holding a short Galil gun. As more and more of them came, we felt the intensity of sex and aggression, the yearning of so many young men at once.

We felt powerful but we knew it was a false power. As women, we were objects of desire, but it wasn't us they desired; we were only a channel through which they expressed their longings. They were yearning for something else: for tenderness, for sanity, for touch, for a taste of the excitement of adolescence. Our goal was to create the illusion that for a moment we could give them all of that. We brought with us a glimpse of home and awakened everything they longed for. While we were used to the impact we had on those young men, their uniforms couldn't hide the boys we recognized inside them. For us, they were men, soldiers, but also our high school friends. We knew that they had many moments when they wanted to cry but had to hide it, sometimes even from themselves. They needed to play the roles they were assigned, to be the men they were raised to be.

I stood on that stage, the lights in my eyes. I couldn't see their faces, only a field of olive. There was a moment of silence before I smiled and said, "Golani, we are really happy to be here tonight." And I started to sing "Naarat Rock" ("A Rock and Roll Girl"), by Yitzhak Laor and Matti Caspi.

When I got to the lines about how the girl had sex with the drummer, I looked back and smiled at the drummer. He wasn't playing the song faster than usual but when it ended I couldn't breathe.

The dynamic between the masculine and the feminine is that the feminine often becomes the container for men's vulnerabilities. They work as a system, and while that dynamic helps one side "get rid" of his neediness and place it in the other, it often leaves him with no real access to his feelings, and with denial of his fear, helplessness, guilt, and shame.

We can see that dynamic in men's relationship to tears, which is often complex. In our culture the split between femininity and masculinity is represented in the split between hardness and fluidity. Heterosexual culture often overvalues solidness, which is associated with erection, masculinity, independence, and activity, while it devalues fluidness, which is associated with femininity, vulnerability, passivity, and even contamination. Being strong is associated with being hard, not being a leaky, needy baby.

That split between the masculine and the feminine presented itself very early in our lives. As a young woman I recognized that when a man comes inside your body, it is potentially a way to console his sorrow, to hold his tears. Love was as intense as war, sex was as emotional as loss, and death was always in the air.

BEN MET HIS wife, Karen, when he was a soldier.

"She used to wait for me at the bus station in Ramat Gan, and as I got off the bus we would hug each other, sometimes standing there hugging for thirty minutes, in the heat, unable to let go. Then we would go to my parents' house, where my mother cooked a big lunch. We ate and then got right into bed. I was always so tired that I don't know how I functioned. I remember waking up the next day, feeling Karen's familiar body, hiding with her under the blankets, and feeling happy. She was my sanctuary. When I came home, I needed her."

Ben's unit was praised for being an effective counter-terrorism unit. They performed undercover operations in urban Arab territories and often disguised themselves by dressing up as locals. They gathered intelligence information and performed high-risk operations like hostage rescue, kidnapping, and targeted killing.

The group was called Mista'arvim in Hebrew, a name that derived from the Arabic "Musta'arabi" (those who live among the Arabs), referring to Arabic-speaking Jews who were "like Arabs," or culturally Arabic but not Muslims.

Ben is not a big guy, and because of his green eyes, long blond hair, and delicate features, he was often chosen to be the one disguised as a woman when they walked into the Arab markets.

Sitting in my office, he tells me about the new Netflix television show called *Fauda*.

"Do you know what *fauda* means?" he asks.

When I shake my head he explains, "That was the code word for being exposed. We shouted, '*Fauda*,' which in Arabic means 'a mess,' to let others know that we needed to run, that we had been discovered. The guy who wrote the show and plays the lead role was a fighter in our unit," he says, "and so much of it is based on real things that happened. I started watching it and found myself thinking, 'What the fuck? This is insane.'"

"And what is it that you watch and think is insane?" I ask.

"I'll tell you the truth," Ben says. "It's that word that you used in our first session: omnipotent. I asked you then what it meant, and you said, 'It means someone who thinks they can do anything, who thinks they have endless power like a superhero, with no limitations. God is omnipotent.' You then said, 'God can't die. People can only play omnipotent and then they pay a price for it.' I remember looking at you and thinking, 'Wow, where did that come from? What is she really telling me about myself?'"

"Yes," I say, "and I remember you then told me about a guy in your unit who, during your first months of training, was reading *Catch-22*, and one day he looked at everyone and said, 'We are crazy. I'm out of here,' and left the unit. And you said that even back then you knew that he understood something that none of you did."

"Yes, he was the sane one even as he seemed so completely insane."

"It was insane to be so sane."

We look at each other and stay silent for a long while. Then Ben glances at his watch, quickly stands up, and starts walking toward the door.

"I'm getting there, Doctor," he whispers. "I'm getting there."

BEN IS TEN minutes late to his next session. He has never been late before and I am a little worried, checking my emails to see if he has written to let me know that he is running late. I wonder if it was the "getting there" from our last session that didn't allow him to get here on time today. Is he anxious about what he is going to uncover or discover? Is he trying to slow down, to communicate with me that we are moving into dangerous territory?

It is not unusual that as people get closer to sensitive emotional material, or even to the issues they came to therapy to resolve, they unconsciously have more resistance to treatment and "accidentally" forget to show up, find themselves late, or sabotage treatment in other ways.

What is it that causes Ben to be late? Is he safe?

There is a knock on the door, and Ben, trying to catch his breath, apologizes, takes his jacket off, and throws himself on the couch.

"You won't believe it, but somehow I found myself involved in a physical fight between two people that I didn't even know," he says. "It was bizarre. Things like that haven't happened to me for years and I don't know what to think."

Ben looks at me and from his expression I realize that I must seem confused or even suspicious. He smiles and points his finger. "I know that look of yours; you squeeze your eyes, I know, it's like you have a question mark on your forehead."

"A big question mark," I say, amused. "I'm glad that you didn't miss it."

"Let me tell you what happened," he explains. "I was riding my bike here and suddenly I heard people screaming and running away from something. I came closer and saw a big guy hitting another, smaller guy. I thought he was going to kill him. And then suddenly the big guy grabbed the smaller one and held a knife to his throat. It all happened fast. It looked like they were fighting over a parking spot and it got out of control. I didn't think and just jumped right in to try to help."

I keep silent.

"It's my instinct, you know what I mean?" Ben is trying to explain. "People shouldn't fight like that; it's crazy. I came toward the big guy and said, 'Man, give me the knife, you don't want to kill someone over a parking spot, believe me, I'm helping you here, give me the knife.' The guy dropped the knife and I quickly stood between them and told the smaller guy, 'Get right into your car. Now!' That guy knew I had saved his life and he ran to the car and drove away as fast as he could. 'Stay safe,' I said to the bigger guy and got on my bike and left. I'm sorry I was late."

I take a deep breath. "That's a good excuse, what can I tell you?" I say, half joking but in fact very serious. "It's hard to argue with a dramatic incident like that. I can see that something made you go right in and not back off. You said this hadn't happened to you for years. Is it possible that it happened now because it is somehow related to getting closer to something emotional here, in therapy? Is it related to us 'getting there'?"

Ben doesn't look surprised or even irritated by my questions. He nods.

"I think you are right. I went there because I was looking for something."

I don't fully know yet what we are talking about, but I understand that Ben needs to get closer to some unprocessed emotional experience filled with aggression, danger, maybe even murder.

"I needed to get in touch with something that I'd rather forget," he says, "but it's haunting me. During the last few nights, I've woken up frightened. Suddenly, I'm having flashbacks."

I look at him and realize that there is still much I don't know about his army operations.

Ben covers his face. I see him thinking, and then he says, "You were right, Doctor, I remember you once telling me that pride is our enemy. If I'm still a teenager, playing superhero, looking for revenge, then I'm not a real man."

"Then you act your feelings, instead of understanding them," I say. "You relive your trauma instead of processing it. I don't know that there is such a thing as a 'real man,'" I add, "but I believe the main evidence for strength is the ability to look reality in the eye. When you are able to do that, you save yourself and the next generation from carrying your unprocessed trauma."

"I know exactly what you mean," Ben says. "My father was a tank driver in the Six-Day War."

IN JUNE 1967, when Ben's father was twenty years old, the Six-Day War broke out.

Ben doesn't know much about his father's experience as a tank driver in that war. "My dad never talked about it. I only knew from my mom, who met him right after the war, that he was fighting in Jerusalem and that his best friend died there right before his eyes."

The Six-Day War was the third big war for Israel since 1948. It was that war that changed the old stereotype of the Jewish male. Israelis were proud of the young men who had won the war in only six days, and a new image of a Jewish man arose. Not only was that man seen as more masculine; he was like King David, able to defeat a greater enemy with his strength.

Yitzhak Rabin, then Chief of the General Staff, announced after the war that it was the *men* who had won the war — not technology, not weapons, but the men who overcame enemies everywhere, despite their enemies' superior numbers and fortifications. He declared that "only their personal stand against the greatest dangers would achieve victory for their country and for their families, and that if victory was not theirs the alternative was annihilation."

The young men's job, then, was to prevent annihilation. This gave them a way to work through the trauma of the Holocaust and the Jews' constant threat of persecution. The men carried the weight of history by adopting a hypermasculine role. At eighteen years of age they had to start presenting themselves as confident and fearless.

"When I was a child I remember my father waking up in the middle of the night, screaming," Ben says. "He was traumatized. Who knows what he had seen. I was born only a few years after the Six-Day War."

In Hebrew, the name Ben means "a boy." When Ben gave me permission to write his story he also helped me choose this pseudonym, a name to disguise his real identity, one that would represent his father's wish to have a first-born son.

"On the day I was called to the army, my father was silent. He walked back and forth and didn't say a word. Then he drew closer to me and whispered, 'No need to cry, boy. You do exactly what you have to do and may God be with you.' He already knew that men were not omnipotent; only God is. He knew where I was going and he was the one who hugged me after a terrible incident. I didn't have to tell him anything, he knew, and he knew that I would never be the same."

The terrible incident that Ben hadn't yet told me about was clearly the moment when he and his father became one. They didn't need, nor did they have, the words to describe their parallel heartbreaks.

"Do you want to tell me about that incident?" I ask.

Ben is silent for a moment. "When I was a young soldier," he says, "I killed someone."

We are both silent.

"It would never have occurred to me that what happened on the street today was related, but when you made that connection I realized that of course it was. We started talking about my army experience, and on my way to you I found myself in a war zone again, this time in the middle of New York City, and I went right in, as if looking for something. Maybe to save someone's life."

Ben tells me about that traumatic day almost thirty years ago. It was hot, and they were sitting on a hill spying on a group of people in the Arab territory. Suddenly it was clear that they were surrounded.

"*Fauda*," someone yelled.

He looks at me and his eyes fill with tears. "I was the sniper. The guy I shot was a little older, maybe in his thirties, and I thought to myself, this man must be a father," he says. "A father," he repeats, now in a firm voice, looking at me as if asking: do you understand what I'm saying?

"I saw him getting closer and closer and I shot him right in the head. Through the rifle's scope I saw him so clearly. I looked right into his eyes and then I saw his head exploding into a million pieces." Ben covers his face and whispers, "It's unforgivable."

I keep silent. There is not a lot to say but to try to bear the pain, the guilt, the intensity of the horror.

"We were proud to be chosen to serve in that unit, teenagers who didn't think about life or death, who wanted to be brave men, not little boys. Only now I'm thinking to myself, what is so wrong about being a boy? Now, when I'm about to have a child myself, it all comes back to me. I wake up in the middle of the night and see the man's face — I can't stop seeing those eyes, I can't stop thinking about his children and remembering what I'd done."

Ben starts sobbing.

"I'm not crying about myself," he says. "I can't fix the past. I'm crying for the injustice. I'm crying for the inhumanity. I'm crying for the children." The tears are streaming down his face.

I am aware of the intermingling of life and death, of past and future, the father he killed and his son, who is about to be born.

Ben tried to fix the trauma and the humiliation of the past. He wanted to be a hero who brings home victory and repairs his grandfather's pride, his father's trauma, and the wounds of history. Instead he was brought right into that trauma. Instead of being only the victim he became both victim and aggressor. Killing another human killed his own soul, too.

"It *is* time to cry," I say, referencing his father in his dream. "There is a lot to cry for. Your father was right."

Ben nods. "I was a boy who thought he was a man. Now I'm a man who is about to have a boy. I will protect my son. You are my witness."

He wipes his eyes as I feel my own welling up. Boy soldiers don't cry. But men, and fathers, can finally begin to mourn.

8

DEAD BROTHER, DEAD SISTER

OUR EMOTIONAL INHERITANCE shapes our behaviors, our perceptions, our feelings, and even our memories. From a young age, we learn to follow our parents' signals; we learn to walk around their wounds, try not to mention and absolutely not touch what mustn't be disturbed. In our attempt to avoid their pain and our own, we blind ourselves to that which is right before our eyes.

In "The Purloined Letter," the third of Edgar Allan Poe's three short detective stories, a letter is stolen from a woman's boudoir. The reader doesn't know the contents of that letter, but we know that it is secretive and forbidden. The police enter the house where they believe the letter is kept. They look everywhere, but they can't find it. As it turns out, the letter is not hidden at all; it is in an ordinary card rack in plain sight and this confuses the police, who expect to uncover a secret truth.

We tend to assume that what we can see must be known to us, but in fact, so much of what we don't know about ourselves lies in the familiar, sometimes even in the obvious. Often we realize that it is in fact right before our eyes, and still we can't see it.

When I meet my patient Dana for the first time, I don't know that her family traumas touch my own. My family trauma is unveiled and brought to life in the space between us. One ghost awakens another, and without awareness that brings us to new places.

My mother's older brother drowned in the sea when he was fourteen years old and she was only ten. In our family this was not a secret, but it was something we never talked about. We all knew that my mother was unable to speak about that part of her childhood. We understood that for her, remembering was a form of living through something that she couldn't live through. The ten-year-old girl that she was had broken into pieces and never recovered. A part of her was gone with him, and only a picture in my grandparents' living room hung as a reminder that many years ago, something was different.

We, her children, were vigilant, trying never to touch what was clearly an open wound, and what became a sensitive spot for all of us.

Once in a while, when someone whistled on the street, we all stopped breathing, waiting for my mother to briefly sigh, "My brother Eli," her voice turning into that of a little girl. "He knew how to whistle, and his were absolutely the loudest." Then she would pause for a moment and change the subject.

In our attempt to protect the people we love from pain, we manage to keep those memories, stories, and facts forgotten, dissociated, hidden in our own minds. We know, and still we do not remember. Our unconscious minds are always loyal to our loved ones and to the unspeakable fact within their souls. So, while something familiar lives inside us, we treat it as a stranger within.

Of course I knew that my mother had lost her brother. Of course I remembered every detail that I had ever learned. At the same time, I didn't know and never remembered. That part of my mother's childhood lived inside me in an isolated capsule, unintegrated with everything else, and when my patient Dana enters my office for the first time and tells me about her dead brother, I look at her tears and don't remember, don't realize in that moment, that she is my own mother who fell apart. I just know I can't breathe.

Dana tells me she wants to start therapy. "But it's not about my dead brother. I'm just too emotional and I need to learn how to control my emotions," she says.

Like my own mother, Dana was ten years old when her brother died in a car accident. Now she is twenty-five.

"How many years can one grieve?" she asks, frustrated that she is crying again.

She tells me that she hated herself all those years for not being able to live like a "normal girl," unable to stop her tears, to ignore the finger-pointing and whispers of "the girl who lost her brother."

She moved to New York City in order to forget, to become someone new. "And besides," she says, "I'm not even sure I cry because of him. I'm just this whiny girl and I need therapy so I can start my life."

"Start your life," I note.

"Maybe I started, but then I had to pause and I'm not sure I know how to unpause," she answers. I see how her fingers tap on the chair as she asks in a childish tone, "Do you know how to unpause a life?"

MY MOTHER'S BROTHER drowned in the Mediterranean Sea. She admired him; she loved his whistles, his jokes, his brilliant ideas.

Dana tells me about her brother. "He was the funniest person in the whole world," she says with a smile, "and I thought I would marry him when I grew up, or at least someone like him." Her eyes fill with tears. It is clear that her pain is still so profound that she can't finish a sentence without a sense of agony. Loss can never be fully processed, but at this point, for Dana, it is an open wound, and every time she thinks about it, the pain is intolerable. I am aware that she needs me to hold her hand and slowly guide her through this land of pain and devastation, but at this point I don't recognize that I am also visiting my own family's devastation.

For fifteen years Dana has been alone with her pain. She has refused to talk with anyone about her past, and that refusal has been a way to protect herself from falling apart. But it has also required her to pause her life. She is frozen in place, a ten-year-old girl who has just lost her brother.

After her brother's death, both her parents became depressed and were unable to function. Her father had to leave his job, and her mother couldn't get out of bed. As is typical with loss, Dana didn't only lose her brother; she in fact lost everything — her family and her life as she knew it. She couldn't bother her parents with her own confusing and overwhelming pain. She tried to make believe everything was as usual and focused on her schoolwork. But she couldn't concentrate, and she failed in every class. "I am stupid," she concluded.

WALKING INTO MY office was frightening and unfamiliar for Dana. Her friend's therapist had referred her to me. She had kept my phone number in her bag for almost a year before she called.

For so many years she had tried not to think, not to know; she had disconnected when she felt too much. It was as if she had been locked in a dark basement, and now we are trying to slowly turn on the lights without blinding her eyes.

It is hard not to feel alone when it comes to pain. To some extent all feelings are isolated, enigmatic, and we transform them, through words, into a form that we can share with others. But words do not always capture the essence of our feelings, and in that sense, we are always alone. This is especially true when it comes to trauma and loss. In order to survive, we disconnect not only from others but also from ourselves. And we cry for the losses — of the people we love, of the life we used to have, of our old self.

Mourning is a private, lonely experience. It doesn't necessarily unify people; it often splits them apart so that they are isolated in their pain, feeling unrecognized, misunderstood, or invisible. We need another mind to help us know our own mind, to feel and digest our loss and everything that we are too anxious to connect to: our shame, rage, identification with the dead, guilt, and even envy.

Dana needs me to know her suffering from the inside, unaware, though perhaps she senses, that in fact I know her feelings better than both of us realize. I don't need to remember my own history; I am living it. I am her therapist, I am my mother's daughter, and I am a mother myself with a daughter and a son. And I witness and identify with my mother and with Dana — a dead sister to a dead brother. All of those roles — some more conscious, some less so — accompany us on our journey.

"In some ways, we mourn forever," I say. My words are an emotional reminder of the fact that the process of loss continues across decades and generations, and that my children and I live with that unprocessed loss, which my mother, still alive today, survived more than sixty years earlier. That grief lives inside each of us, and in that sense, it is part of our family's heritage.

DANA REMEMBERS THE moment vividly. It was just a few days before summer break. Although everyone had showed up for class, it was clear that even the teachers had given up on school. The kids were planning the end-of-the-year party when there was a knock on the classroom door.

My own mother was sitting near the dining room table, doing her homework, staring at her notebook. She was an excellent student and always finished her homework on time. Suddenly she heard a scream. It was her mother's voice, sounding like a wounded animal.

Dana was gazing out the window when she heard the knock. The teacher went to open the door, and Dana saw the nurse whispering something in the teacher's ear. They both seemed serious and then the teacher said, "Dana Goren, the nurse needs you in her office."

My mother heard her own mother yelling, sobbing, screaming, "My son, where is my son? Bring me back my son." The whole neighborhood heard her and people came over and gathered in the house, crying and praying to God that this was all a big mistake. Suddenly, her mother was lying on the floor.

Dana walked silently with the nurse to her office, and as the door opened she saw her parents. They asked her to sit next to them.

"From there I don't remember much. I remember that I didn't really understand what was going on. Everyone was upset and I was invisible. I knew that something terrible had happened."

Dana is crying. I cry with her, and it feels as if this is the first time I have heard something so terrible, so painful, so devastating. It is the first time I have had to think about a younger sister losing her brother, and, in so many ways, it is indeed the first time I have allowed myself to imagine the unimaginable.

Like my mother, I had never let myself think about that experience, to live through it or to feel it. Dana took me to a place where a family secret was buried. Not remembering allows us to keep things "far from home" and to avoid wading into territory that might otherwise be too dangerous. I went there with Dana without fully realizing where I was going, silently following her to visit a hidden grave.

Dana weeps for days, for months. She cries and I sometimes cry with her, explaining to her what she is crying about, how confused and scared she is, how it makes her feel guilty and ugly and dirty. How she had watched her parents fall apart and couldn't do anything. How she had died with her brother.

Slowly, she begins to feel less overwhelmed and starts reengaging in life.

DURING THE LAST year of Dana's therapy, I give birth to my third child, Mia.

"She will have an older brother," my mother cries when she hears the news. I know she remembers herself as a younger sister, and I find myself thinking about Dana.

A few days later I get an email from Dana.

"Welcome, baby girl," she writes to my new daughter. "I'm writing to you, new sister, as a younger sister who has been brought back to life."

PART III

OURSELVES
Breaking the Cycle

PART III is about the secrets we keep from ourselves and about the search for the truth: the exploration of true love, genuine intimacy, real friendship, and the process of healing. It examines the journey we have to take in order to know ourselves, to work through the traumas of our past and to accept our own flaws and limitations as well as those of the people around us. Analyzing the emotional inheritance we might pass on to the next generation is a step toward breaking the cycle of intergenerational trauma. This is the emotional work we do not only for those who came before us, but for our children as well.

The hazard of intimacy frequently plays itself out in families. Parents communicate with their children their ambivalence about being vulnerable. They often either avoid a real intimate exchange or hide behind their wounds and create false intimacy, making their children become their caretakers.

As children, we experience our parents' fears and inherit them, perceiving the world the way our parents did, defending ourselves in similar ways. We are invested in keeping our family secrets but mostly we are trying to keep secrets from ourselves.

What we can't let ourselves know leaves us unfamiliar to ourselves, unable to know others or to be fully known by them. Part III describes the ongoing process of examining our lives, the scars of childhood trauma, and the wish to be better parents than our parents were. It examines conflicts of loyalty as they appear in romantic relationships, between parents and children, and in women's friendships.

The growing ability to integrate and process pain helps us find meaning, heal, live life to the fullest, and raise the next generation with honesty and integrity.

9

THE TASTE OF SORROW

It is rare that I find myself taken off guard by a patient's secret. But I was not prepared for what I discovered after Isabella's death.

I have never met Isabella. She was my patient Naomi's best friend.

It isn't unusual for therapists to feel that we know our patients' friends, lovers, and family. In some ways, we accompany those people from afar, as if they were characters in a beloved book. We will never meet them but we know them intimately and have feelings for them. We get attached to the people in our patients' lives; we follow their stories; we watch them change with our patients and see their relationships develop or sometimes end.

Naomi has been in therapy with me for three years, and that is how I have come to know Isabella, who has been her best friend since childhood. Both of them grew up as only children, and in some ways they have been sisters to each other.

Naomi takes a tissue from the box on the side table. She is shaken. She tells me that Isabella has just been diagnosed with ovarian cancer and that the doctors don't know yet how bad it is or if it's treatable.

We are both silent.

Isabella gave birth only a few months earlier. She always wanted a big family, and when she learned that she carried BRCA1, the so-called breast cancer gene, she and her husband decided to rush to have another child. Then she would have the surgery that she believed would save her life, a double mastectomy.

"Now it's too late," Naomi says quietly and immediately adds, "But Isabella is brave. If anyone can make it, she can."

I recognize the way Naomi comforts herself, using her idealization of Isabella.

Naomi and Isabella met when they were nine years old and both joined a musical theater group after school in the small town where they grew up.

"Isabella was one of those girls you couldn't miss," Naomi told me in one of our first sessions. "She was beautiful even as a little girl and behaved as if she knew she was talented and attractive and didn't need others for reassurance. We all wanted to be close to her, tried to be her friends, wished to be her."

In fourth grade, the musical theater group performed *Aladdin,* and Isabella got the lead role of Jasmine.

"No one was surprised," Naomi said, amused but also a bit annoyed. "Isabella wasn't only talented; even as a young girl, she, like Jasmine, was a princess who believed in love and fought against injustices. All of us were envious of her freedom to express her opinions; she wasn't afraid of adults and didn't obey authority."

Isabella refused to accept the lead role. She stood up to the director and said it wasn't fair for her to play Jasmine because she was a new student and the role should go to the kids who had been there longer.

"She wasn't scared," Naomi said again, and I knew that she couldn't recognize Isabella's fear that was hidden in that act of rejecting the lead role. In thinking about her own life, comparing herself to Isabella, Naomi could only see her friend's boldness. She felt paralyzed, unable to own her life.

It is not always clear who gets the lead role in Naomi's life. Sometimes it feels as though she gave that role to her mother, sometimes to Isabella, as she silently accepts the supporting role. When speaking of her childhood, Naomi describes her parents as a perfect couple and her mother as good, charming, beautiful, and caring. It often feels as though she is left to witness her parents' love from the outside. She admires her mother and her parents' relationship. Naomi finds a way to play out that childhood dynamic with Isabella, whom she idealizes.

Naomi had decided to start therapy because she felt unhappy but didn't have any idea why. During our first session she described how she grew up in a loving and stable family and told me about Isabella, who — unlike Naomi — was raised by a single mother in a volatile household. She told me that Isabella was the one who constantly searched for answers, while she, Naomi, didn't even have any questions. Now she was looking for something but she didn't know what.

Even in Naomi's own treatment, at times Isabella became more important than Naomi. In my writing of Naomi's story, once again, Isabella's story often takes over. This recurrent enactment brings us into the heart of Naomi's hidden struggle with knowing and being known, with feelings of inferiority and competition. Naomi and I wonder whom and what we actually know and what is used as a way to hide.

"I DIDN'T SLEEP last night," Naomi opens the next session. She looks distressed. "Isabella called me late and in a very matter of a fact way said she wanted me to come over as soon as I could. She said that she needed to tell me a secret."

Naomi pauses and turns to me. "We were always so close and I didn't think we had any secrets. It worries me. What is it that she wants to tell me?"

My thoughts are racing as we sit together in silence for a long minute.

"I'm meeting her tomorrow," Naomi says, trying to allay her fears. "It will be okay. I feel honored that Isabella wants to share her secret with me." She smiles and adds, "Do you know that I have always been her secrets keeper?"

In high school Isabella spent most days and nights at Naomi's house. Once in a while she told her mother that she was at Naomi's but instead stayed over at her boyfriend Sam's. Naomi was happy to be Isabella's alibi. After all, Isabella was not only her best friend but one of the most popular girls in their grade. She was the student council representative, she was on the volleyball team, she sang and played guitar in the school's band, she knew how to put on makeup before anyone else did, and she was the one the boys loved the most.

Sam was Isabella's first boyfriend. They were in tenth grade when Isabella shared with Naomi that she was in love with Sam, a popular boy and the captain of the varsity basketball team. When they kissed for the first time, Isabella ran to Naomi's house to tell her, and a few days later she showed Naomi the note Sam wrote her. *I can't stop thinking of you.* He signed it with a heart, and they were both excited.

Isabella and Sam were a couple for a few years. He was the first guy she had sex with, and she shared that secret with Naomi, her best friend. When they graduated high school, Isabella and Sam broke up and went to different colleges.

When they were in their twenties, Isabella had one boyfriend after another, passionate love affairs, which Naomi followed, always a little jealous and feeling slightly betrayed when Isabella prioritized her boyfriends over Naomi. She wanted to be loved the way Isabella was, but instead — as in her relationship with her mother — she was a witness to someone else's love.

One day, when she was in her twenties, Naomi ran into Sam on the street. She called Isabella right away to tell her about it. She asked her if she would give her permission to go out with Sam. Isabella didn't mind. She was in love with another guy; she gave Naomi her blessing. A few years later, Isabella was a bridesmaid in Naomi and Sam's wedding.

Now, in her late thirties, Naomi looks back and tries to understand why she isn't happy. I listen as she begins to unpack her relationship with her mother, her friendship with Isabella, her marriage with Sam.

"What am I missing?" Naomi asks again, sounding desperate. It is clear to both of us that she has worked hard to keep herself from knowing the truth about her life and about the people around her.

"I know it's a cliché," she says apologetically, "but life is short." I'm aware that Naomi is referencing Isabella's illness, which brings her in touch with the fragility of life. She feels frightened and disappointed.

"On the surface I have everything I ever wanted and I love my family, but I feel so defeated, as if life were supposed to be something else, more than what it turned out to be. Now Isabella is sick and it makes me angry." Naomi's voice becomes louder.

"Sometimes I feel that I don't know anyone at all, not even Isabella. I feel betrayed and I'm not sure why."

I know what Naomi means. Naomi views Isabella, as well as her own childhood and her perfect mother, in ways that often don't feel real. She idealizes the world around her as a way to protect herself from seeing things as they really are. It's not just that she doesn't know others; she is afraid to discover herself.

Idealization is a defense mechanism that serves to keep the illusion that things, or people, are perfect, and even better than reality. It is based on the splitting between good and bad, which children do in order to organize a safe and predictable world. As we grow up and become less fragile, we allow ourselves to see the world as more complex. As adults, we sometimes use idealization to pretend that things are perfect, that people are not flawed and that we don't have any negative feelings or ambivalence about them.

"I always wanted to be like my mother. She was everything I wanted to be." Naomi looks at me and adds in embarrassment, "But I failed."

I recognize how similar those feelings are to how Naomi feels about Isabella. In her idealization of both women she splits between good and bad and perceives them as all good and herself as a failure. This is her way to defend against feelings she can't tolerate having about them and about herself. Naomi can't let herself know how ambivalent she feels about them, how envious she can be, how angry. Rather, she directs those negative feelings toward herself.

"She was always better than I was. She was beautiful, smart, talented, and I was myself. I know it's childish but I feel like pointing at my mom and saying, 'It's not fair, it's not what you promised me.'" Naomi takes a deep breath and then says with annoyance, "My parents loved each other; they were the perfect couple. Doesn't that mean I am supposed to be happy in my own marriage? Isn't that how it works?"

I pause and wonder if I should state the obvious. "It sounds like you felt inferior, maybe even unworthy compared to your mother."

Naomi looks intrigued, as if my words force her to recalculate everything. I continue: "While our parents' relationship can serve as a model for our romantic life, it is usually our relationship with them that we repeat in later intimate relationships."

Naomi seems startled and I'm worried that maybe I have just put into words the forbidden — that which was known but not allowed to be spoken.

"Unworthy," she repeats my word. "I remember that when I was about ten years old I told my mother that I didn't believe they loved me the way they loved each other." Naomi sighs and continues. "My mother got so upset. She said that I shouldn't talk like that, that of course they loved me, and that one day I'd grow up and have a love exactly like theirs." Naomi stops and looks at me. "But I never did," she says. "Sam loves me, but he has never loved me the way he loved Isabella. She was his first love."

Naomi tries to hold back her tears. She doesn't want to cry but she can't help it. "I hope you know how much

I love Isabella," she says. "I feel devastated. I feel awful to compare the two of us right now, when she is so sick."

Isabella is fighting for her life while Naomi is trying to figure out her life. Isabella's illness forces Naomi to face the excruciating limitations of our existence: that nothing is all good or lasts forever, that we are all flawed and vulnerable, and that bad things happen to everyone, even those we idealize.

Before she leaves, Naomi asks to meet me again tomorrow, and we schedule a session to follow her breakfast with Isabella.

Naomi leaves and my heart is heavy.

THE NEXT DAY Naomi comes in and immediately throws herself on my couch. Her eyes are red. She doesn't speak and just sighs.

The news is bad.

"It was brutal," Naomi finally says. "Isabella is dying." She bursts into tears.

So many questions are running through my head, but I keep silent.

"Isabella gave me packages with things to give each of her four children after her death," Naomi whispers. "That was her secret. She didn't want anyone to know about those packages."

"How heartbreaking," I say, and Naomi tells me about the packages.

"It all started when Isabella read about a woman who, when she learned she was going to die, prepared several years' worth of dinners for her family. For a few weeks that woman cooked every day," she says. "She packed all the meals in boxes, and labeled them with dates, and stored them in a big freezer."

Naomi takes a deep breath. "Isabella said she regretted that she was never a good cook. 'Can you believe I might force them to eat my cooking for years?' she joked, and I pretended it was funny."

They laughed together, and Isabella shared with Naomi her idea of leaving something for the children, letters and gifts for important events she would miss. They both knew that like that mother she read about, Isabella couldn't imagine separating from her children.

Naomi doesn't look at me. "Many people recover from cancer and she could be one of them," she says. I realize that she is trying to calm herself, to make sense of everything, to feel less helpless.

She continues. "'Don't think about it,' I told Isabella. 'You are about to start a new experimental treatment. There is still hope.' I held her hand as tightly as I could. 'Isy, you are a fighter. It's not over,' I said.

"Isabella didn't answer. I could see that she was irritated, but she kept silent and just handed me four big blue boxes. She asked me to go over her directions, to make sure I understood what to do with them.

"'Open on your eighth birthday,' she wrote to her daughter on a big square envelope. On another, 'Open on the first day of school.'

"There were good luck notes, gifts, and letters for birthdays and graduations. She left each of the girls a book on puberty, the same book she and I used to read together when we were twelve years old. It was so painful that at some point I stopped and couldn't go on. 'Isy, why?' I wanted to ask, but she was determined and I knew that I should do what she wanted me to do; that if she could handle it I should be able to handle it too."

Naomi and I sit in silence. There is no real way to escape the pain, and words cannot capture it.

"Before I left her house Isabella seemed restless. I felt like she was trying to tell me something but couldn't, and I have to admit, I'm not sure I wanted to know. It was already a lot." Naomi shakes her head. "I feel like such a bad friend," she says. "Isabella needed me to imagine with her how it feels to say goodbye to her children and know that she will never see them again. She needed me to know that they will need her and that she won't be there for them. And I just couldn't. I wish I could put my selfish pain aside and help her. I wish I had the courage to ask her what else she was trying to tell me."

Naomi leaves my office and I'm glad that she is my last patient of the night. Walking home, I listen to the familiar hum of the city, which like the white noise machine in my office helps me to daydream when I'm alone.

The Bowery neighborhood in Manhattan is never peaceful, and its hectic rhythm allows my thoughts to flow freely. I feel a strong urge to rush home and hug my own kids, to hold them tight and not let them go. I remember that feeling from when they were babies, how I used to hurry back, imagining our reunion — their smiles, their smells.

Instead, I end up wandering. I walk aimlessly around the Bowery, back and forth on the same route that I take every day from my home to my office, and I cry. I cry for Isabella. I cry for her young children. I cry for Naomi and I cry for what I know Naomi doesn't know about my life: that my life partner, Lew, is sick with bladder cancer and is fighting for his life.

I walk on the street, carrying my patient's pain, my own pain, not knowing yet that sooner than anyone expects, Isabella will die, and that not so long after, on a cold February morning, I will lose Lew to cancer.

I find myself gazing at a group of young people waiting outside for a table at a trendy new restaurant. The days when I used to be one of them seem far away. I look at them with longing and see only purity, innocence, naïveté. They all look so happy, so glamorous, as if they have never lost anyone, never felt devastated or realized that cancer could be waiting around the corner, unaware that they might lose everything they have.

Splitting, that primitive defense mechanism of all or nothing, takes place again, as it does in moments of devastation, dividing the world into good and bad, those who suffer and those whom we believe don't know pain. And we look at them with wonder and envy, the healthy people who we imagine don't know the taste of sorrow.

For Naomi, I'm one of those people. She needs to see me as immune, invulnerable, as living outside the rules of reality in which we are all survivors or survivors-to-be. It helps her see me as strong enough to be with her, but nevertheless that need to see me as pain-free leaves her alone again, connected to idealized others and with the feeling that no one can truly know her.

"I feel so alone," she says, and I share with her the feeling that we all need another human to bear witness and accompany us on the emotional journey of life, another person who can accept our feelings and process them with us. We need to be known.

When Naomi was a child, her pain wasn't recognized and thus she couldn't make sense of it and had to deny it. The emotional holding that parents provide for their children is about accompanying them in their lives, giving names to their feelings, helping them tolerate the intense emotions that come with being alive. Now Naomi gets in touch with her loneliness, conflicted about trusting that I could understand, aware of her worry of knowing too much about her own pain as well as about Isabella's.

It is only when we process our own sorrow that we can offer a truthful space of mutual vulnerability and emotional honesty, a place where we can recognize the other and don't try to know better, to fix or give optimistic advice. Instead we are available to be with, listen, and bear our own pain with the pain of another human.

In the last few weeks of Isabella's life, Naomi sits with Isabella's family next to her hospice bed, holding her hand.

Isabella's older child goes to school and acts as if nothing is happening. It is always confusing to witness the way children deal with loss, to understand the things they are worried about that may sound trivial ("Who is going to put me to bed at night?") and not to confuse their dissociated state with lack of care or to blame them for being selfish. Grief is a tricky and unpredictable creature. It changes its face every minute and often appears in disguise. In some ways, in those unbearable moments, we are all children who need someone to tell us that there is life after death.

Lying in her bed, Isabella becomes more and more disconnected.

"I feel far away," she tells Naomi. "I looked in the mirror today and I felt that I had already left."

Naomi tells me about her guilt and the pain of separation. "She is agitated and angry," she says. "I constantly feel that I have done something wrong, that I could be more helpful, that I could do it better."

I know that Naomi's guilt is about being healthy and alive. It is about not being able to save Isabella and abandoning her, sending her all alone into the unknown. But it is also about feeling so abandoned and devastated.

Isabella dies on a Monday morning when no one is there.

"She was waiting for us to leave," Naomi says.

Naomi is left to process her losses, to count her regrets, to cherish their friendship, and to wonder how she can move forward.

"Can you believe it really happened? I lost Isabella. She will never come back." She sobs and I cry with her. I feel that I have lost something as well. But mine is an unusual, unrecognized loss. I grieve for a woman I have never really known and mourn every loss I have ever experienced and cry for the losses of my future.

THE NEXT DAY is rainy. On most mornings as I walk to my office, I listen to the voice mail messages on my cell phone. This morning, I'm holding an umbrella in one hand while trying to hold the phone close to my ear with the other.

I rarely accept new patients these days, but something about the message I hear strikes me as unusual. I listen to it again.

"I need to grieve but I don't know how," the caller says. Intrigued, I call him back and we set up an appointment.

The following week a man in his mid-forties walks into my office.

"Hi," I say, referring to him by his first name. He smiles. I look at his face and try to find a sign of his loss.

"The woman I love just died," he explains, after he settles into the couch. "I felt that I needed to speak with someone and a friend gave me your number. I'm not even sure where to start."

I nod and he continues. "Her death was sudden. From cancer. One day she was here, and the next she was gone."

He lifts his head and looks into my eyes. "She left me many notes," he goes on, "a box filled with love letters. I'm not sure why she thought that might help. It only makes it worse."

"She left you a box of letters?" My voice is too loud.

"A big blue box," he says. "That's just who Isabella was."

"Isabella?" I hear myself say.

"I mean, the woman I was with," he clarifies. "We were lovers. We had a secret relationship and we both tried so hard to end it, to go back to our lives and forget each other. She even had a baby with her husband to try to stay in her marriage. But our love was stronger than life. We decided to have a life together right before she was diagnosed. A couple of months later she was dead."

I can feel my heart beat as he continues. "She was the love of my life, but strangely, ever since she died I find myself thinking I just made her up, that she never actually existed. Do you know what I mean?"

He looks at me, and I can see the tears in his eyes — and feel tears building up in my own.

"Love needs a witness," I say. "I know what you mean."

I'm thinking about Naomi and her devoted witnessing of Isabella's life. I'm thinking of everything I know that this man doesn't realize. I'm thinking of the major role this man played in Isabella's life and of his painful loss. So many invisible characters, so many secrets.

I decide to refer him to another therapist. He deserves his own separate treatment, and Naomi deserves my loyalty. I want to cherish her Isabella and not confuse her with the Isabella of the man I've just met.

I am left stunned to process my own feelings, holding

more secrets than ever. Is this the secret Isabella wanted to share with Naomi, or did Naomi know this and keep it as a secret from me? I may never know. I'm reminded of the enigma of the human mind, questioning whether we can ever fully know another person's pain.

10

THE CYCLE OF VIOLENCE

One snowy day, Guy, a man in his mid-forties, walks into my office for the first time. Wearing a heavy gray coat, he nods and says softly, "Like you, I am not used to this weather."

I am not sure exactly what he is referring to, and I wait for an explanation.

"I was born in the same city you were born in," he continues, almost whispering.

We switch to speaking our mother tongue, Hebrew, but very quickly I come to understand that we are speaking different languages — one innocent, the other dangerous.

"So," Guy says slowly, as he tries to find a comfortable position in the armchair. "How come you chose to become a psychoanalyst when no one else in your family is in the mental health profession?"

That is strange, I think to myself. How does he know no one in my family is a therapist? And if he doesn't know, why would he make those assumptions? But I don't have to speculate long, as Guy goes on: "Your sister, she is an architect, and her kids seem pretty sweet."

He doesn't assume, I realize with fright. He knows.

"It looks like you know a thing or two about me," I say, inviting him to clarify, maybe to confess that indeed we met many years ago in Tel Aviv, or that we have mutual friends who referred him to me.

Guy smiles. "I'm sure I know more about you than you want me to know," he says. He pauses and then adds, "I hope you enjoyed your summer vacation in Italy."

How does he know that? I start getting anxious and annoyed. Who is this guy? Why is he here?

People usually start therapy curious to learn more about themselves than about their therapists — at least initially. Having said that, most of my patients do come to their first session already knowing at least a little about me. They google me and can easily find a picture, my age, my birthplace, and my professional affiliations. Some dig deeper and discover something about my personal life, my musical background, or the obituary of Lew, my life partner. In our digital age, the classical psychoanalytic idea of neutrality is challenged. Whereas in the past our goal as therapists was to stay objective and make sure our patients couldn't know anything about us — not even from our office decoration — nowadays we work with the information people inevitably have about us, and we search for the unique meaning this has for each patient.

The preliminary information patients have on their therapists contributes to a fantasy about who their therapists are and what therapy is going to be like. Most patients, however, limit their search so they don't learn more than they want to know or can handle. I assume that those who have a negative reaction to my online profile wouldn't contact me, and I'm sure some patients might know more about my personal life than they tell me, or even more than I let myself realize. Most patients, though, do not disclose their online research, especially not in the first session, and they come with a wish, as well as a dread, of being known by me.

Guy introduces a different dynamic. I'm aware that he needs me to feel that he has invaded my private life.

"Are you worried?" he asks. "I'm not sure, but you don't seem happy that I did this research about you."

"Did you think I would be happy?" I ask.

He shrugs. "I am not a stalker or something, I hope you know," he says. "I just needed to find out. These days, who knows, strange people are everywhere. I wanted to make sure you are not some lunatic. And I kind of like that your father was born in Iran. It's pretty interesting."

I look at him and wonder: Why would he want to make me so uncomfortable? My professional self should know the answer, but I feel paralyzed, unable to think clearly. I remind myself that Guy surely wants and needs me to feel the way I feel: unsafe, even frightened. He needs to make me feel at least as intimidated as he feels when he walks into my office, perhaps as alarmed as he has been every day of his life.

I'm not sure what Guy is afraid of. But I am aware that I don't yet have his permission to explore that question, that I'm not invited into his world, and instead that he has invited himself into mine.

Confusing the therapist with intense feelings, evoking fear, or even presenting intense erotic fantasy can serve as a defensive strategy to make sure the therapist is unable to think, and therefore unable to know anything real about the patient.

What would happen if I were able to think, to put things together, to make connections and discover who he really is? What might I, or he, discover that Guy needs desperately to hide?

The British analyst Wilfred Bion writes in his paper "Attacks on Linking" about the ways in which people try to avoid knowing anything that is too much for them to tolerate, to evade the painful truths of their lives. In therapy, they unconsciously attack the psychoanalyst's ability to work. Instead of investing in making connections and meaning, they make sure no links can be made — links between ideas and feelings, between past and present, between therapist and patient. Connections then are replaced with disconnections, so that patients can escape the pain of discovering themselves.

Guy enters therapy feeling too exposed, and he makes sure to project — to instill that emotion in me. Now I am the one who is fearful of being invaded by a dangerous stranger.

"You really worked hard to find out all of these things about me," I finally say.

Guy smiles again. "It's not hard for me. That's how I live my life. I pay a few people and they give me all the information that I need."

"You wouldn't start therapy with someone you didn't fully know," I note. "I wonder why. What would happen if we ended this session with me knowing more about you than you know about me?"

Guy looks disappointed. "What do you mean?" he says. "You already know more about me than I intended." He takes a deep breath. "Maybe it's strange, but I feel that you know me."

We look at each other silently and then he glances at his watch. "I think our time is up," he says as he stands up, grabbing his coat. "This is mind-blowing," he mumbles. "I don't know what to think."

He holds the doorknob, turning to look at me again before leaving, and says, gently, "Now that you know me, do you think therapy is for me?"

Guy leaves before I have the chance to say anything, and I realize that we haven't made another appointment.

Two weeks go by and I don't hear from Guy. Frankly, part of me is relieved. I recognize that since our session I've been a bit restless and I try to understand why. I find myself thinking of Guy when I am out walking, and I look around to make sure no one suspicious is following me. When I am on my phone, I have the fleeting thought that he might be listening. And I have the urge to google his name and learn more about him. Maybe he is a criminal or some secret agent, I think. "And besides," I hear myself repeating his words, "these days, who knows, strange people are everywhere."

I'm able to make sense of my thoughts and remind myself that paranoid thinking by nature is contagious. People can evoke fear in each other in unpredictable and powerful ways and without awareness. That unconscious force is one of the reasons conspiracy theories and fear are so easy to spread. It is why leaders can easily frighten people by pointing to the enemy and promising them they will be protected and saved.

Guy was right, I think. In that one session I really learned something profound about his internal world and especially about how threatened he feels.

As the days pass, I become more and more curious about the feelings I'm left with. When Guy reaches out again, I offer to meet him for one more session and only then decide if we would like to start working together.

It is a cold day in March when Guy comes to my office for the second time. He greets me and asks to keep his coat on.

"It's crazy outside," he says, and points at the window. "What the hell? I'm telling you, climate change is going to kill us soon."

"Yes, it's scary," I say.

"It's more than scary," he replies. "It's a catastrophe. It's out of control and we will find ourselves dead very soon."

Many of my patients speak about climate change, but Guy sounds a little different. His fear seems immediate, as if he is currently struggling to stay alive.

He sits down.

"We did it to ourselves. We destroyed ourselves," he

concludes. "Actually," he then says angrily, "it's them. They fucking did it to us."

"They?" I ask.

Guy looks right into my eyes. "It's their fault," he says. "Generations of people who didn't take care of the planet. Our parents, our grandparents, our great-grandparents. They created this disaster with their own hands and now we have to deal with it. What a mess. There is no way we'll be able to fix it; that's the problem."

Like Guy, I find the situation disturbing and worrisome. But I'm aware that even as we agree, the words one chooses always have their roots in one's personal history. The political intermingles with the personal. I listen to Guy's words and try to recognize what it is that he is telling me about his life, about his fears and his pain.

"The destruction the previous generations caused, the struggle they put us in — you know something about that," I say.

"Obviously," he answers, though he doesn't elaborate.

Guy communicates with me that he can't rely or depend on anyone, not the people who raised him and not anyone since. He is in my office, asking for my help, but is worried that I can't be trusted. I look at him, sitting with his heavy gray coat on. He leans back on the couch and his eyes wander, searching the room.

"Did you actually read all these books?" he asks, but doesn't wait for an answer. He points at the picture on the wall behind my chair, an abstract painting on a big canvas.

"Interesting," he says. "What did the artist mean?"

The picture Guy points at is the only one in my office that I painted myself, and it has been hanging there for the last fifteen years.

"Those dogs," he says and points at the blurred figures in white and yellow. "They are running away, don't you think?"

"I see what you mean," I say.

"They are like me," he says, laughing. "Running away."

"What are you running away from?" I ask.

"I was just kidding," he answers. "You know, we all ran away. You live in New York. I live in New York. This is not our home, but we are here. This city is filled with ambitious survivors who ran away from something. Everyone here has something they wanted to escape."

Guy takes off his coat.

"It's kind of pleasant here," he says. "It's not too cold but also not too warm, do you know what I mean? In the winter, people heat their apartments so much that you think you might die. But you did a good job. It's exactly right here."

Guy feels less threatened, expressing the hope that I will do a good job and be right for him. He uses projection again, a defense mechanism that places threatening thoughts and feelings outside of the self. Through projection we deny anxiety-provoking feelings and instead put them in others. Uncomfortable feelings such as anger or sadness tend to be projected into other people in order to get rid of them. When a person is, for example, angry, she will attribute those feelings to others and be convinced that the other is angry at her, when in fact it is her own anger that she feels. I'm remembering Guy entering my office for the first time and how he filled me up with a sense of fear of being invaded, a feeling that he instilled in me and thus effectively communicated the sense of danger he lived with himself.

Similarly, paranoid thinking is often understood as the projection of aggression onto other people. Our aggressive impulses make us anxious and we often try to feel better either by overcompensating with kindness or by projecting those feelings onto others. Paranoid thoughts are a result of our aggressive feelings, feelings that we couldn't tolerate and needed to get rid of by attributing them to another person. The more aggression is disowned and projected onto others, the more frightened we then become of those people.

Guy feels too anxious to talk about his feelings and instead talks about the world around him, placing his feelings outside himself. He is hesitant about taking off his coat lest he would be too exposed, too vulnerable. He makes sure not to create a coherent narrative, and I sense that there is a secret behind his smile.

"Why are you here, Guy?" I finally have the courage to ask.

Guy stays silent for a long minute.

"Because I come from mental illness," he says. "I might be mentally sick too."

I'm not yet sure what he means, but I see how he is taking the first step toward me, toward a new future.

Guy looks at his watch and then puts his coat on.

"It's enough for today," he says, and I notice that he is the one ending our session again. "I'll see you next week," he says as he exits.

IT IS THE beginning of summer and a few months since Guy started his sessions with me. We now feel more comfortable with each other and I have learned to appreciate Guy's cynical sense of humor and respect his ways and his rhythm. Guy often needs to avoid direct conversation; he rationalizes and intellectualizes his feelings and speaks in general terms. While I know his opinions about many topics, he tells me very little about his past or his family.

Every Monday evening I wait for Guy to arrive. He is never late, and now, five minutes before his session, I hear the doorbell ringing. Before I have the chance to answer it, it's ringing again, and then again.

I open the door and Guy storms in and immediately closes the door behind him.

"How did you know who's at the door?" he asks, still standing at the threshold. "How did you know that it was me ringing and not some random person who wants to break in?" He sounds anxious.

"You are worried," I say, and Guy doesn't answer.

We both sit down. I notice that he doesn't carry his usual backpack. He hasn't gone to work, I assume.

"Your doorman doesn't seem so effective; he is sort of sleepy," Guy says, and I hear him sigh. "Today I had jury duty and it was such a long day."

"And what made you think about my safety today?" I ask.

"I'm not sure. I walked here from the subway and I saw a man downstairs. He looked strange. He seemed violent, something about the look in his eyes." Guy points at the window. "He was here, on the street right at the entrance of your building," he says. "I suddenly thought that this man could get into the building and ring your doorbell, and you could buzz him in, as if he were me. How would you know?"

Guy is hypervigilant, constantly detecting activities around him and anticipating threats and danger. That sensory sensitivity is usually the result of early trauma. High alertness aims to predict and prevent danger, and the more

I know Guy, the more I recognize the scared little boy hidden underneath. That boy is frightened; what if I open the door, assuming it's him, and another guy shows up and hurts me? The threat is from both outside and inside — the man outside is dangerous and Guy is afraid he, too, might bring the danger with him into my office. He is threatened by the violent other, and I know that it is also his own unconscious aggression that he is worried might sneak into the room. The aggression from the outside and the aggression from inside him are intermixed, confused, as it always is when a child is exposed to violence early in life.

Guy seems overwhelmed. I wonder about his childhood, why he is especially susceptible today to what seems like an activation of an early trauma.

"Was there anything in jury duty that made you feel unsafe?" I ask.

"Not at all," he answers. "It is a case of a father who broke his daughter's arm. The police have been involved, and the girl and her mother, the man's ex-wife, got an order of protection against him. I mean, I'm not sure why he is in court. What else do they need from him? The man can't hurt her anymore." Guy looks at me and then continues. "The daughter is sixteen years old and she posted her story all over social media, saying awful things about her father. It feels wrong. It's messy," he concludes. "I have such bad luck. Can you believe that this is the case I have to deal with?"

"Traumatic," I say.

Guy looks confused. "Kind of," he replies. "I mean, the man is an asshole, that's for sure, but is he a bad person? Is he the monster his daughter describes? I don't think so." He pauses and gazes out the window.

"What did you think just now?" I ask when he turns to me again.

"I don't know," he says. "I guess I'm not sure how I feel about this. There is a noise in my head. I wish I could stop thinking. I mean, it's clear that she hates her father so much and I feel bad for him," he continues. "She wrote on Instagram that she wishes he were dead. I guess I understand that part. I used to wish my father were dead."

"That makes sense," I say, carefully stepping into his childhood.

While most kids are afraid of losing their parents, I've often heard patients describe that as children they wished for their parents' death. The parent is the one the child depends on for survival; that wish usually surfaces when the parent is the one threatening the child's physical or emotional being. The wish helps the child feel less helpless as she imagines she can make the parent disappear. It expresses the child's pain as well as rage — two feelings that are fused and confused. The child simultaneously feels helpless and is overwhelmed with anger that she can't process. Abused children often have difficulty regulating feelings. Love and hate intermingle: the people you love are also those you hate.

I notice that Guy becomes flooded with emotions. He needs to take a break.

"It's sick," Guy says. "It pisses me off." He suddenly stands up. "Excuse me, I need to use the bathroom," he says. "I'll be right back."

He comes back a few minutes later, smiling. "Did you notice that I said 'piss' and then went to pee?" he jokes. "You see, I know how to therapize myself."

He is conveying that I have taught him something, but also that he is not dependent on me, that he can do it on his own. The ability to master and control his life is crucial. It's the only way he feels safe, and he needs to make sure that he is in control in our sessions as well. I'm again aware that it's Guy, not me, who ends each session. When he feels overwhelmed, rather than turning to me for comfort, he withdraws.

"I needed to be alone for a moment, to calm down," he says. I know that there is something about jury duty that awakens his childhood trauma. "As a child, I spent hours in the bathroom. My father used to lock my brother and me in there every time he got angry, which was all the time. He would lock us in there for hours, and I learned to sit on the floor and wait. And I thought to myself, I hate this man. I wish he were dead."

Guy doesn't look at me. "You know," he says, "sometimes, when my friends came over and we made noise, I would suddenly hear him calling my name. I knew he was angry and that he was going to lock me in the bathroom again. I had no choice. I had to do what he told me to, or he would yell and hit me in front of my friends. He locked me in while they were waiting in my room, wondering where had I disappeared to. It was humiliating."

Guy tells me about his childhood for the first time. His face is serious but he doesn't express any emotions. I listen in silence.

As he is speaking, I slowly notice that I start feeling pain in my body, and I sense an urge to change my position in the chair. I watch Guy turning uncomfortably in his chair and wonder what it is that we each feel in our bodies.

"No wonder you needed to run away," I say, remembering his interpretation of the blurred figures in my painting. "Your wish to run away was an act of hope."

Guy nods. "As a child, there was nothing I could do. I had nowhere to go, no one to turn to," he says quietly. He explains that his mother was afraid of his father and couldn't protect him and his brother.

"My only hope was that one of us would disappear; either he would die or one day I would leave everything and escape, find a new home in another country. I would flee to a place where no one could find me," he continues. "Like my mother, who always seemed so frightened, I learned to hide, to be silent, to make sure I was invisible." Guy looks straight into my eyes. "I don't know how to explain this to you," he says. "My father is a sick man. You have to understand, it's not his fault. That's how he grew up, that's how his parents grew up, his grandparents. He didn't know anything else and he believed that this was the right way to raise his children. I'm not angry at him."

I hear Guy's conflict. He is trapped between identifying with his father and wanting to be different from him. He doesn't want to be angry because anger will make him too much like his father. But he empathizes with that father in court more than with the man's daughter.

Anna Freud defined "identification with the aggressor" as a defense mechanism that children use in the face of abuse. The victims, instead of only feeling threatened and helpless, try to make sense of and control reality by adopting the abuser's beliefs and behaviors. By impersonating the aggressor, the child turns passivity into action and instead of being just the victim, she becomes the one who hurts others and/or herself. These children, in identifying with their parents, believe deep inside that they deserve the parent's anger and punishment.

It is not surprising, then, that like Guy's father, many violent parents were once abused children. Guy doesn't only feel angry; he is still trying to make sense of the world around him and to figure out who is bad and who is good. Unprocessed abuse keeps the intergenerational cycle going. Each generation identifies with the previous one, and Guy is at a point where those intergenerational conflicts have come to the surface. He is torn between his loyalty to the past and the hope for the future, between the connection to his ancestors and the chance to have new and different kinds of relationships. As in his childhood, he is imprisoned again, but this time he is the one who locks himself in.

Healing — breaking the cycle of abuse — is often filled with resistance to the possibility of change. That possibility intensifies the conflict between the part of the self that strives for future liberation and the part that is connected to the past and to previous generations. Healing is a journey filled with ambivalence, guilt, and shame. It is a painful process that brings the ghosts of the past to life and challenges our internal identifications on the way to setting us free.

Guy stops and glances at his watch. "I don't want to talk about it anymore," he says. "What's the point of talking about it now? We can't change the past."

He starts gathering his things from the side table. Holding his keys, he looks at me and says, "Galit, at the end, I did save my life. I'm here in New York almost twenty years now. I was able to run away."

I know that it will take time to process all the feelings that are brought up to the surface. Guy moved to New York in an attempt to survive, but his past chased him — as it always does.

He puts his keys back on the table. "We still have five more minutes," he says. "I have to go to jury duty again tomorrow. I wish you could come with me." He starts laughing. "I'm just joking. I wouldn't want you to have to hear that girl describing her childhood. It's brutal."

"I know our session today was brutal," I say, "and I assume you always wished for a mother who could come with you and protect you, make you feel safe, and help you to be brave."

He glances at his watch again. "Our time is up. Maybe I should come another time this week," he says, taking another step toward rather than away from his pain. He *is* brave, I think.

We plan to meet again on Thursday.

THAT NIGHT I have a dream. Guy and I are in a big castle. We are both wearing miners' helmets and each of us is holding a flashlight as we go down the stairs to the basement. We are clearly looking for something.

"I brought you here to save my brother," Guy says. "He is in captivity."

The castle is dark and I'm worried that we have gotten lost. Guy says he is frightened. "Let's run away; it's filled with ghosts here," he says.

"We have to be courageous," I hear myself saying, either to him or to myself.

The ghosts of the past control Guy's life. I am aware that he and I are on a journey to revisit his trauma and listen to the little boy he used to be, the boy he left behind when he ran away in order to save his life. Now we need our flashlights to illuminate everything that he left down in the basement of his life, everything that prevents him from moving forward, living, and truly loving.

Thursday is a warm day and Guy walks in smiling.

"Do you see how different the weather is from Monday? I'm telling you, life is so unpredictable. My mood has changed, too. I'm sorry that I was so emotional on Monday." He looks at me and suddenly starts to giggle. "You just had such a funny expression on your face," he says. "I bet I know what you had in mind," he continues, his tone playful and tender. "You thought, 'What are you apologizing for, silly boy?'"

I smile, aware of the maternal feelings I have for him and realizing that he has recognized these on my face. He is right; I was wondering what he was apologizing for.

"You let the boy you used to be have a voice on Monday," I say. "It was the first time I have heard that boy. He is sensitive, vulnerable, traumatized."

"He was in captivity," Guy says to my surprise, conjuring the image from my dream. "I couldn't wait to come here today. I wanted to tell you that I did something big." He pauses, and before I have the chance to ask what he means, he adds, "At court on Tuesday I voted guilty for that father." He sounds proud. "I looked straight into his eyes and for the first time in my life, I didn't feel fear. I thought about you and said to myself, 'You know what? It's not me who should feel bad. It's him.'"

We sit in silence. I know how hard it was for him to go against the father, and how painful it is to let himself remember his childhood and protect the abused child he once was. Guy had wanted to "bring" me with him to court because he never had a parent who would defend him, and therefore he was worried he wouldn't be able to defend himself.

Guy breaks the silence. "I feel embarrassed remembering how as a child, I used to hide in my room, trying not to make any noise, not even to breathe so my father wouldn't notice me. I hated myself for being weak like my mother and not protecting myself, and for feeling angry, like my father. And I felt ashamed for hiding while my older brother, Ram, became my father's main target." Guy pauses and looks at his watch. "Ah — we have a little more time," he notes.

"You know, the other night, after I came back from court, I had a thought. I realized that Ram, my brother, was that girl, the daughter."

"In what way?" I ask.

"Like her, he fought back; he wasn't afraid. I watched him from the sidelines and I felt jealous that he was so brave; but I also felt guilty that he was the one my father attacked, while I was able to hide. And then one day, when Ram was maybe fifteen years old and almost as tall as my dad, he came home from school with a girl, and my father got angry and smacked him in front of her. Instead of apologizing, which is what I would have done, Ram slowly walked toward him. He put his finger on my father's forehead and whispered angrily, 'You. If you touch me one more time, I'll kill you. Do you hear me?' My father stepped back and Ram walked away. I think it was the last time my father hit him. I remember my mother and I walked away too, as if nothing had happened. It was unbelievable, how they switched roles and my brother became the aggressor. I remember that I suddenly felt sorry for my father. I almost wanted to help him. How fucked up is that?" Guy's voice becomes louder. "When I turned twenty, I left. I'm sorry. I had to leave. I just had to," he says angrily.

"What are you sorry for?" I ask.

"What do you mean?"

"You just said 'I'm sorry' again."

"Did I?" Guy looks at me, startled. "I guess I did. I guess I feel that I have something to apologize for, don't I? Maybe I feel bad that I ran away and left them all behind. A family of sick people. I saved my life, but what about them?"

The loyalty to the people we are attached to often keeps a part of us with them even when we leave. Our parents tend to live inside us without our permission. Our relationships with them are the first we have, and our future relationships exist only in dialogue with them.

Guy had to move away but he still struggles with the guilt of leaving — and living. As I have come to learn from him over time, he hasn't been able to create a safe-enough home in New York or to have an intimate relationship. He isn't sure that he can love or trust others, and he certainly doesn't trust himself to protect the people he loves from his legacy of brutality and abuse. Being alone feels like the best way to hide, and hiding, after all, is the only way to survive.

In our first session, hiding behind his gray winter coat, Guy told me that he had researched me, wondering about who I was and about the people I had left behind. He questioned if therapy was even for him: Could he have an honest relationship, where he felt known, without being too vulnerable or threatened? Could he heal the abused boy he once was without feeling humiliated and ashamed? Could he ever love and be loved?

On a snowy day, one year after Guy started his therapy, he walks into my office, nods, and says softly, "I think I'm getting used to this weather."

He takes off his coat and smiles. We both notice the difference.

11

THE UNEXAMINED LIFE

ALICE LOOKS YOUNGER than her age. Maybe it's her long black hair, or maybe it's the sweatpants and sneakers she wears to our first session that make me think of her as a girl. She comes to see me right after celebrating her forty-fourth birthday. Very quickly her age becomes a topic.

Alice was in her late thirties when she met Art, I learn. It was right after she got divorced, and she was worried that she might be too old to have children.

"I don't care about marriage," she tells me in that first session. "My parents separated when I was five years old. They had a messy divorce and after my father officially remarried, he was not in the picture anymore."

I ask her what she means by "officially remarried."

Alice rolls her eyes. "It's not why I came to therapy, but I guess it's all relevant to what I'm dealing with," she says. "I had a shitty childhood. Again, it's not why I'm here."

"Why are you here?" I ask.

"We are about to have a child," Alice says, and I'm a bit surprised because she doesn't look pregnant at all.

"We tried to get pregnant for years. Between you and me, from our first week together we knew that we wanted to have children, but I couldn't get pregnant. I tried everything. Many cycles of IVF." She turns to me. "Do you know how expensive that is? Our whole family helped us financially. My mother and her husband gave us their savings. Art's sister gave us money too. I'm embarrassed to tell you how much. You sit in the clinic's waiting room, you look around, and you think, 'All those privileged people; I guess I'm one of them now.' So you can imagine how awful it was when it didn't work. Not only could I not get pregnant; I couldn't even make it happen by paying a fortune. That's what I call bad genes."

"Just a second." I try to slow her down to make sure I follow her. "So you were married in your twenties and didn't have children; then in your thirties you got divorced and met Art and tried to get pregnant right away — "

"Exactly," she cuts me off. "Art and I were both married before, but our love was like nothing we had ever experienced. It was very intense from the first day we met. I'll tell you about it one day."

"And you are here because you are about to have a child," I say.

"Exactly," Alice confirms. "Another woman is about to give birth to my child."

"A surrogate mother?" I assume.

"Yes. We got an egg donation too. It's not my biological child. It's a girl, by the way," she adds, making sure I have all the information, but I can't find where she is emotionally.

Alice continues. "So you see, there are three women involved in the creation of this baby: an egg donor, a surrogate mother, and me — at this point a woman without a role. The fourth person is Art. This child is going to be his biologically. Did I tell you that he has a daughter from his first marriage? Lili. She is amazing, so we know that he has good genes." She smiles.

"Oh, and one more detail," Alice continues. "Since we had already emptied everyone's bank accounts for the IVF, we still needed to figure out how to pay for the surrogacy. We took a loan out but it is *insane*. I'll tell you about that too."

"There is a lot to talk about," I note. "How are you dealing with all of this?" I ask as I try to get closer to the emotional struggle I believe Alice is here to explore.

She doesn't answer.

"I don't know, actually," she then says quietly. "I am not sure how I feel about it. Some days I am disappointed with myself. I feel damaged, that I'm a failure and I'm not going to be anyone for this baby. On other days, I feel relief. First, because being pregnant and giving birth doesn't sound like fun. It doesn't feel like something I'll be sad to skip. But the real reason, and I know this sounds awful, is that I would rather have a child who doesn't carry my genes. It's probably better for her."

I ask her to tell me more. "Why wouldn't you want her to have your genes?"

"I come from pain," Alice says. "It's in our DNA. Bad luck and trauma. My mother had the most painful childhood, like a bad movie. Her family immigrated to the United States when she was around eight years old, and her mother died on the way. They had to carry her mother's body until they got to a place where they could bury her. My mother was probably sexually abused by her grandfather but no one in my family talks about that. You see, when I say trauma, I mean real trauma. I have never been in therapy before. My mother has never been in therapy either."

"So you are here for both of you," I say.

"Exactly," Alice answers. "Maybe if she could have stopped this cycle of misery, I wouldn't be so worried about raising another miserable woman-to-be. The last thing I want is to have a daughter who inherits the bad luck I inherited from my mother."

"Another miserable woman," I repeat her words.

"Exactly," she says. "My mother would never admit she is miserable. That's why she became a hippie, if you know what I mean. She always has a smile on her face. She believes that we should focus on our own healing and spiritual journeys. Meanwhile, she was never happy. She had a traumatic childhood, two failed marriages, a failed career. When I was a child, she was at home with me all day. She used to say how much she loved it, and that she brushed my hair so many times, she became an expert in brushing hair. I always had long curly hair that was hard to brush and I hated it when she said that. I sensed her resentment. I remember one day at a school gathering, the parents were asked to introduce themselves. My mother, with a sweet smile on her face, announced, 'I'm Alice's mom and I'm a professional hair brusher.' I wanted to die." Alice looks at me to make sure I recognize her mother's hidden bitterness and especially the ways it was concealed behind a smile.

"Meanwhile, every time she could disappear for a few days she would. She would leave my stepbrother and me with my stepdad and go on retreats. When she came back home, she'd sleep with my little brother. For years I believed that she was putting him to bed and falling asleep there because she was tired, but as I grew up I realized that she just didn't want to sleep in bed with my stepdad," Alice says. "My mother never admitted that she didn't really love my stepdad, that he was a compromise. She needed a husband because she was too frightened to be alone. I feel so bad for her for not having the life she wanted. I used to blame my stepfather for that. I guess I wanted him to make her happy so *I* wouldn't have to."

Alice speaks fast and hardly takes any breaks. She plays with her fingernails. I notice that she bites her cuticles until they bleed.

"Don't get me wrong. The main person I blamed for destroying my mother's life was my biological father," she continues. "I hated him. My mom, by the way, was never angry at him, not after she found out that he had had an affair, not even after he had left her for that other woman. She used to say that he broke her heart and that his abandonment of her hurt so much because it was a reminder of her own mother's death when she was eight years old. My mom never got over what happened with my dad. He was awful. Did I tell you that he had another family?" she says and glances at her watch.

I find myself out of breath. Alice keeps talking and I am overwhelmed with feelings that I don't have a moment to digest. I assume that I am feeling what she has always experienced. She helps me get to know her from the inside when, like her, I feel overloaded with information. I have no way to stop things from happening, to understand, or to process the information.

It is the end of our first session and I'm left with many questions. I recognize the implicit connections Alice makes between her mother's traumatic past, her own bad luck, and the wish to save her unborn daughter from the same future.

Alice and I plan to meet twice a week.

ALICE COMES BACK a few days later and to my surprise but also my relief, she picks up where she left off. I wonder how she felt about our first session, a question I often ask in second sessions. But Alice communicates with me a sense of urgency. She sits down quickly and immediately starts talking.

"Basically, my father had another family," she says. "He had children with that other woman, and when my mother found out, he left us. I'm not sure how she found out exactly, but you can imagine how traumatic that was for her. This is where we ended last time, right?"

I nod. "Last time you told me about your mother's past," I say. "And how your father's abandonment was a reminder of her early loss of her mother. You described her dissociated anger and how you felt so angry at him for her."

Alice seems puzzled. "I guess that's right," she says, and I'm aware that I framed it in a way that felt new to her.

Alice starts exploring her identification with and profound loyalty to her mother, who was the parent who raised her.

"She is a brave woman who carried a lot of pain but still was able to forgive him and even pray for his happiness," she says. "She was a bigger person than he was. And you know, after she found out, her family used to call him 'the monster,' but she would ask them to stop. She would say that she was sorry she wasn't a good enough wife and didn't give him what he needed. For years, that made me so angry. I saw the sadness in her eyes and her struggle to recover from his betrayal. As a teenager, I swore that I would never speak to that man, that I would never forgive him. And honestly, she was the one who tried to convince me that he was my father and that I had to try to understand him. But the more she said it, the angrier I became.

"'I'm not interested in this motherfucker,' I would say, and I would never return his calls.

"At first, he would call me every day. I was only five years old and we spoke for a minute because my mother forced me to. Then, when I was in middle school, he would call once a week and I'd say that I was busy and wouldn't call him back. At some point he stopped calling. He had a new life with that woman and it felt like I didn't exist for him anymore."

Alice keeps talking. She tells me about her childhood, and the angrier she gets, the sadder I feel.

"Did I tell you that about a year ago I reached out to my father?" she asks. "I think I was ready to hear his side. He was excited to hear from me and super nervous when we met. He said he would do anything to stay in touch with me and to repair our relationship. But the truth is, there was nothing to repair. What I realized by then was that he wasn't my father anymore. I'm a grown-up now, and he missed my childhood. He is just a stranger who has nothing to do with me, except biologically." I see Alice thinking and then she adds, "I hope you know that my mother never pushed me to reject him. It was my own choice."

For the first time, Alice begins to recognize what she lost as a child. She was protective of and loyal to her mother and estranged from her father. As a child Alice thought fathers were not important. She wasn't jealous of her friends who had good relationships with their fathers and believed that as long as she and her mother had each other, they were better off without him.

Unconscious dynamics are, behind the scenes, shaping Alice's life as a repetition of her mother's history. While she believes she inherited her mother's genetic "bad luck," it is in fact the identification with her mother, and the unconscious attempt to heal her mother, that bring Alice to live the same psychological pain her mother experienced:

the drama of a daughter who loses a parent. Her mother's trauma is reenacted in Alice's childhood and, like her mother, she, too, grows up with one parent and loses the other.

Alice's loss, unlike her mother's, was not framed as a tragedy for the daughter. Through this reenactment, Alice and her mother could relive the mother's history together, but this time with the illusion of control; Alice believed that it was her own choice to end the relationship with her father. Instead of feeling sad, like her mother, she felt angry. Instead of being abandoned, she was doing the abandoning. Alice and her mother shared an unconscious fantasy of repairing her mother's trauma and healing her.

Alice's loss of her father remained unrecognized and even dismissed. Once again, grief and sadness belonged solely to her mother — her mother was the one who had lost a husband she loved, and Alice became her emotional caretaker, replacing the mother her own mother never had. It is only now, for the first time, that we start questioning how much choice Alice actually had in that family dynamic as we try to differentiate between her mother's needs and her own.

"My mother remarried but she was still unhappy. Her childhood trauma was always there and it made her fragile and sad. She never stopped mourning her mother, and she never recovered from my father's abandonment of her."

Alice is unconsciously tied to her mother's traumas. I recognize how confused she feels as she tries to find out the truth about herself and the people around her. Her parents were both dishonest, in different ways, and she struggles with the double messages she received from them, with her mother's dissociated anger, with her father's lies, and with her own aggression, which functions as a defense against her hidden vulnerability.

Alice pauses and searches her pockets. She finds a hair tie and quickly puts her long dark hair up in a ponytail. Then she looks at me and smiles.

"My mother is almost seventy years old now and she wears her hair in two long braids, like a little girl. Did I tell you that?" she asks.

In that moment a thought crosses my mind. I wonder if her mother was envious of her for being a child with a mother. Does her mother need to keep herself looking like a young girl with the hope that one day she, too, will have a mother who will take care of her and brush her hair?

It is not unusual for mothers who didn't have mothers themselves, or those who had abusive mothers, to resent their daughters for having the mother they never had. In therapy, the mother often explores feelings about her daughter having more than she had; she envies her daughter for having her as a mother.

Trying to understand Alice's mother's psychology, I become aware of how, in our sessions, I switch from analyzing Alice to analyzing her mother, and I assume this is my unconscious collusion with Alice's enmeshment with her mother. I'm enacting her wish to heal her mother and to make her stronger. In these moments, I become her mother's therapist — her mother's mother — as Alice fantasizes about being able to leave her mother with me to take care of while she goes off to start a family and become a mother herself.

"I can't afford to hurt her feelings," she says. "Maybe she can have sessions with you too. Maybe she can work on her trauma, because if I try to talk to her, she immediately tears up and says, 'I did my best to be a good person and a good mother.' And you know what? I believe her. She *is* a good person and I love her. I know she did her best."

Alice's mother needs to feel she is the victim and not the cause of the traumatic events that happened to her. To be a good person means not feeling angry. Alice, on the other hand, feels better when she is not a victim. She would rather be angry than sad. That disparity in their defenses is Alice's attempt to be different from her mother, to be an active agent and control her life.

"I'm trying so hard to be different but I am too similar to my mother. That's exactly the problem," she says. "The breast milk I drank was hers and it shaped my body and my mind. I didn't belong to anyone but her. I didn't have a father. My stepfather was an outsider and it was only my mother and me in the inner circle. Yes, I hate to be a victim but I, too, had a really sad childhood. I, too, got divorced. My luck is so bad that I can't even get pregnant from having sex, like everyone else. I need to go through hell. And I want everyone to leave me alone, just as my mother wanted. She wanted to leave us and go on her retreats. I want to protect my baby from the same future. She will have Art's genes; he is amazing."

Alice takes a deep breath. "Now you know why I'm here." She finishes the sentence in a childish voice.

We are left with the clear link between the past and the future, the previous generation and the next one, and with Alice, in the middle, trying to bridge the two, to heal her mother as a way to liberate herself, to make sense of her past and to create a better future.

THE BABY WILL be born in two months and Alice feels unprepared.

"Maybe I started this process too late," she says. "I have so many things to tell you and to talk about before she arrives."

I wonder out loud about her urgency to resolve everything before the baby is born.

Alice is frustrated. "You have no idea," she says. "It *is* urgent. There are so many decisions I have to make. And I suddenly have many feelings and so many bizarre dreams at night. I'm worried about the money and how we are going to cover that loan.

"They say that money isn't important," Alice continues, sounding upset again, "but have you noticed that the people who say this are usually the ones with money? Money is in fact very important when you need it and don't have it."

I think about the open way Alice talks about money. Sex and money are two topics that people usually try to avoid, not only in their lives, but in therapy too. Those subjects are filled with hypocrisy and dishonesty, and therefore they're a good place to hide other feelings and needs that people are uncomfortable expressing. Any unwelcome feeling can be expressed through sex or money: aggression, hostility, the need for domination and power, as well as fragility, narcissism, and trauma.

Sex, for example, can be seen as lovemaking even in cases where it is a way to express hostility. Like money, sex can be used to control others, to compensate for emotional insecurities, and to express or hide pain. Avoiding talking about money and sex allows us to disguise any negative feelings. In therapy, for example, negative feelings toward the therapist could be expressed in delayed payments.

When we are too embarrassed to talk about money, we might miss the opportunity to reveal and process feelings that the patient wants to hide.

Alice talks about the cost of the reproductive process and explores her feelings about everything she might not be able to afford, financially but also emotionally. The enormous economic burden is part of a broader weight of self-doubt and shame that she carries.

When reproduction involves such transactional or medicalized aspects — when it happens away from the couple's bed — it often breaks the romantic fantasy of a baby born "out of love." Difficulty getting pregnant can bring to life, in different ways, intense shame, and evoke the darkest fears and feelings about being damaged, cursed, rotten, broken, or bad. It is a profound injury that touches an essential insecurity about one's body and existence.

Like many people, Alice struggles with the feelings that her inability to get pregnant might be a sign that she is not supposed to have a baby, that she doesn't deserve it, and that she won't be a good mother. She tries to push those painful feelings aside. She sees herself as damaged with bad genes and defends against her disappointment. While disappointed in herself, she is preoccupied with the ways she disappoints others, especially, as I come to learn, the surrogate mother.

"I feel like she wants me to be involved in this process but I constantly forget to call her. I feel guilty that I don't care about her or the baby. I've heard that some people talk with their surrogate every few days. I call her only once in a while. What am I supposed to ask her? How is she feeling? Sure, I can do that, but it would be fake. I don't really care to hear the details about how she is doing. The most difficult decision I have to make now is whether I should be there when she gives birth. I mean in the room," she clarifies. "What do you think?"

"I think it's hard to have someone else carry and give birth to your baby while making believe that it's only easy and happy. It evokes a lot of feelings, positive and negative. It can be insulting and disappointing," I say.

"Exactly," Alice agrees. "Finally someone understands. People don't get it. They say how happy they are for me and how exciting it is that we will have a baby soon, as if it's all good. A friend told me the other day, 'The minute you have the baby, you don't remember how it came into the world.' What nonsense." Alice sounds angry. "People are so stupid, or maybe they just feel bad for me and try to console me. But that's dishonest and it makes me feel totally invisible. Like they don't see what I'm going through. Also, I feel absolutely weird about being in the room with her when she gives birth. I wouldn't want some woman to be there, looking between my legs, if I were giving birth. I want to give her privacy. I don't know. How do you think she feels? What do other people do?"

I believe Alice is afraid that it might be too painful for her to witness another woman giving birth to her daughter.

"I think you are worried about what you might feel there, in the delivery room," I say.

"I'll be an outsider," Alice states. She is silent for a moment and then adds, "Now I understand how fathers feel. They don't carry babies inside them, they don't give birth to them, they don't breastfeed them. Nothing. That brings me to my next dilemma," she continues, and then she presents one of the questions many women in her situation struggle with.

"Should I take hormones so I can breastfeed the baby? What do *you* think?"

I follow the connections Alice makes between being an outsider and being a father. She said that she and her mother were the inner circle. Her father was an outsider. I recognize that her current conflict is related to the historical fact that, for her, the only way to love is to be a mother, not a father. She struggles with the fear that not being able to give birth to or breastfeed her child implies that she is a father rather than a mother. The problem of gender binary doesn't allow fluidity in her perception of herself. It activates the shame of not being a "real woman" and, hence, the fear of becoming her father instead, whose love she couldn't trust.

"Are you worried that you won't be able to love your baby?" I ask, making the explicit link between gender and love.

"Absolutely." Alice nods. "How do I know that I will be able to love her if I don't give birth to her and breast-feed her? I'm not so sure a parent can love a baby without those love hormones. I mean, nature has arranged it so that women immediately produce oxytocin."

"It's as if you believe that love hormones are what make a parent love their child," I say.

"How upsetting," Alice whispers. "I thought I got over that. What's wrong with me? Like my mother, I'm stuck being a little girl, still thinking that her father didn't love her, even though I know it's more complicated than that." Alice sighs. "I see what you are saying: that underneath my wish to breastfeed my baby, I worry that I won't love her the way 'real' mothers do, which was the only love I trusted."

"Exactly." I hear myself using her words.

Alice looks at me and I notice her holding back tears. "My father left me and he never came back. The angrier I was, the more he withdrew, until he gave up on me. He didn't call anymore. He just sent me a birthday gift once a year with a card that read, 'Happy Birthday, my girl. I love you forever.' I thought he wrote that because he had to, and that deep inside he didn't really care. He had a new life with the woman he left us for, new children, and a new house. I'm not sure why I'm crying. I didn't care about him anyway."

Alice is sobbing. She cries for the father she lost years ago, for the little girl who believed that her sad mother was the only one who could love her. She mourns her inability to carry and give birth to her baby. Alice is filled with fear that she won't be able to love her newborn, and we realize that she feels like an unlovable girl herself.

"What if she doesn't know that I'm her mother?" She wipes her tears. "What if *she* doesn't love *me*?"

There is so much pain buried inside her, sadness that she is used to covering up with irritation and anger. She doesn't want anyone to know that just like her mother, she secretly mourns. She doesn't want her daughter to have to experience her grief, the way she carried her mother's grief. She knows what a burden that was on her, and she is worried that her daughter will have to live that legacy.

"I TOLD ART about our session," Alice says when she walks into my office the following week. "We had a long conversation about breastfeeding and hormones, and it's like I had another session with him after my session with you." She adds with a smile, "Victory. We made a decision."

Alice pulls a bottle of water from her bag. She places it on the table. "Do you notice how anxious I am?" she asks. "I want everything in place before our baby is born. And I made the decision that I won't take hormones. One thing is crossed off my list and it's a relief, so thank you."

"Tell me more," I ask. "How did you make that decision?"

"Suddenly, it wasn't a hard decision to make. I told Art that I realized my wish to breastfeed was based on the fear that I wouldn't be able to love the baby without those hormones. I told him how upsetting it was for me to realize that I doubt myself as a woman, and that under the surface this was about my feelings that my father didn't love me. Art knows the whole story, and a lot has changed between my father and me since I met him. I think he helped me to see my father as a full person. You will appreciate this," she says playfully. "I think I fell in love with Art when I realized how afraid he was of losing his daughter, Lili, in his divorce. Isn't that a good psychological link?" she asks with a smile. "He was the father I never had, and I betrayed my mother for the first time when I fell in love with him," she says. I ask her to explain.

"It was as if my mother and I had a secret contract that *we* were the family. Even when I got married the first time, my marriage was similar to hers — not a big love but what she thought a woman should do. I was married, but I was still hers. We planned that if I had a baby I'd move to live closer to her, and she would help me raise my child. It was like she was my partner. But then I met Art, and it was a double betrayal." Alice looks at me to see if I can put it all together.

"A betrayal because you actually fell in love with him and he became your partner instead of her," I say. "But what else? Why double?"

Alice closes her eyes. She speaks without looking at me.

"When I met Art he was still married. That's why. I had just gotten divorced and Art had already left his marriage, but he was not legally divorced. One thing I thought I knew for sure was that I would never, ever be with a married man. It was against everything I believed; it's wrong, as a principle. So I tried to stay away from him. But it was hard. We worked in the same company and at some point were assigned to work on the same project. We had to speak every day and ended up spending hours on the phone. Our conversations became more and more intimate. Art told me about his separation and how hard it was for him. He had Lili, who was five years old at the time, exactly the age I was when my father left, and he talked about how painful it was for him not to spend nights with her. I told him about my father and how he cheated on us and left for another family. He was the first person I shared all the details with. I even told him about the ceremony my mother conducted."

"The ceremony?" I ask.

Alice opens her eyes and looks at me. "Right, I forgot that I didn't tell you about it. It's a weird story. I was in first grade, and my father had already left but they were not yet divorced. One Sunday evening, my mother drove me to his office. I had been there many times before with my dad, but that evening was different. She opened the door with a key that she still had from when they were together. His office looked exactly the way I remembered it. My father is an accountant, and his office was on the second floor of a brownstone in town, about an hour from where we lived."

Alice closes her eyes again as she continues talking.

"My mother needed a goodbye ceremony. She explained to me that we had to move on with our lives, and that in order to do so we needed to have a healing ritual that would allow us to let go. She didn't cry but I remember that she looked so sad. When we walked into his office, my mother stood right in front of his desk. She said out loud that she wished him the best in his new life, and then she took off her wedding ring and placed it on his desk.

She collected the framed pictures of our family and put them in her bag. Then she pulled from her bag a small sculpture of a bird that we used to have in our living room. It was a gift he gave her before they got married. She put it on the shelf next to his desk. On his chair, she left their wedding album along with some of his stamp collection albums, which he had forgotten to pack.

"Before we left, my mom said that she had one last thing to do. She stood in the corner, holding a few cards, and I recognized his handwriting on them. I think they were birthday or anniversary cards he had given her through the years. She whispered some things that I couldn't hear and then spread them out on the floor.

"When we got back to the car my mother asked how I was feeling. She said that we were free now and that this healing ceremony had already made her feel much better. I remember saying that it made me feel better too, but I was lying. That night I couldn't sleep. I cried but I didn't know why.

"Art was the first person I ever told this story to. I remember his silence on the phone. And then I realized that he was crying. I asked him why he was so emotional, and he said he was not sure if it was because this was just a very sad story or if he was identifying too much with my father and felt his sadness at losing me. I was so touched by that answer and by how kind he was in his attempt to hear my story and not mix it with his own. It felt like he was the first person who ever considered my feelings."

Alice's voice becomes tender as she continues. "It was also the first time I thought that maybe my father *was* sad. That maybe he had lost something too. I know it sounds strange, but honestly, I never thought about how he felt when I didn't want to see him anymore. I never imagined how he felt when he walked into his office that Monday morning. It didn't occur to me that maybe my mother did this to hurt him and not only to heal herself. Even when I say it now, it feels wrong. I don't think she had bad intentions."

I hear how through Art's eyes, Alice's view of her father became more nuanced. She could start seeing him and her mother as complex humans who struggled to survive.

"After about a month of nightly conversations with Art, when we talked about absolutely everything, I agreed to meet him outside of the office. And that was it." Alice pauses. "We spent that night together and knew that we would spend every night of the rest of our lives together. A month later we tried to get pregnant."

"And you felt like you were betraying your mother," I say.

"Oh yeah," she replies. "I obviously told my mother right away and she was happy for me, but I knew that I had crossed some secret line. I was afraid to tell her that he wasn't legally divorced yet. I was afraid she would see that as a move toward my father and would worry that I might forgive him and leave her. So I told her gradually.

"At first she just listened, as she always did. She was always a good listener. And then she asked, 'Is he a good man, Alice?' And that made me so uncomfortable because I knew what she really wanted to ask. I knew she was thinking about my father. But she didn't want to ruin it for me. She just kept asking if he was a good man.

"'Why do you keep asking that, Mom? Of course he is,' I answered, and she noticed that I was irritated.

"'I love you more than anything,' she said. 'I want you to be with a good man. I want you to be happy. One day you will have a daughter and you will understand that.'"

Alice looks at me. "To tell you the truth," she says, "it did ruin it for me. It made me worried. I felt her doubt and I thought that maybe she could see something about Art that I couldn't. When I was with him, I felt completely safe, but when I was with her, I felt her suspicion of him, and it made me doubt my own judgment."

I wonder out loud if it was her fear of losing Alice that made her mother so worried.

Alice seems intrigued. "You know what Art likes to say? That it's impossible to separate from my mother. For him, the most fascinating thing is my father's choice of creating another family behind my mother's back instead of leaving my mother when he wasn't happy. My dad left only when my mother found out and he had no other choice. I mean, don't get me wrong. You'd have to be a real asshole to do something so immoral, but Art was fascinated by that choice. He said that for someone who was not a psychopath it must have been so much more difficult to lie like that and live a double life than to leave. And trust me, it was very hard for Art to leave his family, so it's not like he was saying any of that is easy.

"I see things differently now. I see how my father was unable to leave her because he couldn't handle hurting her. Does that make sense? I'm sure he couldn't even tell her how unhappy he was in the marriage because she would feel so awful. I'm not blaming her, but I'm sure he knew he would lose me if he left her, and he was right. He was a coward, and she controlled him with her sadness, I guess the same way she controlled all of us."

I recognize that Alice needs to be able to find a way to accept both her mother and her father, with all their imperfections and faults, so she can accept herself with her human limitations. She needs to become her own person, free to choose, as opposed to a daughter who is trapped in her parents' world.

I hesitate at times, questioning whether understanding her father is in fact obedience to a normative structure, not a form of freedom. Is there a real freedom in the acceptance of both her parents, in the forgiveness of her father? Or is it only a way to conform to the patriarchal order in which men systemically have more power, and thus fathers are not judged as harshly as mothers? I sit with the questions that fill me, as I see Alice struggle to break that binary of identification where she has to be like her mother or like her father and is only allowed to be loyal to one of them. I know what a burden it is on her and how it keeps her as a little girl with no real power to choose or to grow up.

Alice grabs the water bottle and puts it back in her bag. "Therapy is tiring, you know?" She smiles. "I never knew that I had so much to talk about. Do you have other patients like me, who talk and talk and don't let you get in a word?"

I smile. I like Alice and I know how hard it is for her to talk about her childhood and to challenge her narratives the way she does.

"I feel stronger," she adds, and I nod in agreement.

"It's like I'm giving birth to myself," she says proudly. "And you are my midwife."

WHEN I OPEN the door the following week, I hardly recognize Alice. It takes me a minute to realize that it is her hair. She has cut it short.

"What do you think? Do you like it?" She sounds excited. "The other day I asked myself what I would want to change before my baby is born. By the way, we decided to name her Zoe, which means life."

Alice looks a little older. I think about her decision to name her daughter Zoe and to cut her hair, which she mentions in the same breath. I recall our conversations about hair: her mother's long braids, which seem inappropriate for her age; her own long curly hair, which was hard to brush; and her mother's resentment of the brushing.

Zoe will be born soon. Alice will become a mother and she doesn't look like her mother anymore. Cutting her hair is a symbolic way of cutting the thread, separating before becoming a mother herself, and by doing that, allowing her daughter to have a life of her own, free of the legacy of trauma.

Before I have a chance to share any of these thoughts, she turns to me and says, "I have one more thought from this weekend. Tell me what you think. I want to consider accepting my father's offer to pay for the surrogate mother."

"Tell me about it," I say, thinking about the new haircut and this development. Alice is working to reorganize her family structure. She tries to challenge the mother-daughter–centric family in order to make space for a multimember family. I'm aware that this is enacted in her process with me as well, where Alice has made sure a third person is symbolically with us in our sessions. At first it was her mother, whom she constantly analyzed, and then it was Art, with whom she shared our sessions. Alice was unconsciously trying to avoid the dyadic experience that most people seek in therapy, where patient and therapist become an intimate therapeutic couple in a private, secretive process. Instead, what Alice needed was to create a triangle that first included both her mother and me and then included both Art and me. She needed to create a structure in which she didn't have to be loyal to only one parent. That dynamic revived the original family she had lost as a child but was also a rehearsal for the family she was about to have.

"Art and I had a little fight about it this weekend," she says, and I am aware that it's the first time I've heard of them having a conflict. "I think I told you, a long time ago, when I told my father about our infertility and the IVF and everything, he offered to pay some of the bills. I was shocked and immediately said no. I was worried that he wanted to bribe me and I didn't want him to control me. So even though we didn't have the money, we took a loan from the bank instead. But my father didn't give up. He kept saying that he wanted to be part of this process. I told him I'd think about it but I never got back to him."

"Like in your childhood." I cut her off, and she nods.

"This weekend, Art and I talked about my childhood. I told him that in therapy I realized that I always dismissed my father's attempts to be close to me. I just didn't trust him. I told Art that I see things a little differently now. He understood what I was saying but he said that I still don't let my father into my life and that when he tries to give me something, I reject him."

Alice smiles. "You know how Art speaks like a parent sometimes? He is smart that way."

I hear her slight ambivalence about Art's parental position and I smile and nod.

Alice laughs. "I know," she says. "He can be annoying the way parents are sometimes. He argued that parents feel good just being able to give their child something she needs, and that it's not always just a power move, the way I usually interpret it. He said that financial support is one way for parents to express their love. He talked about love languages and how each person has their own way of showing love, some through words and some through actions, and that one way isn't better than another.

"I started to raise my voice and said that my father's actions are not something he should be proud of. He cheated on my mother as a way to express his unhappiness, which I don't respect. I said that I'd rather he express his feelings in words, not in actions. Art said that I'm totally wrong and that, in fact, it's the act of loving that counts, not just the words or the feeling. He argued that people are truthful when their words and their actions are synchronized, and that my father's act of betrayal was awful because his words and actions contradicted each other. But that doesn't mean he is not allowed to try to repair it with a loving act. Art thinks my father is trying to give me money as a way to tell me that he wants to make up for everything he did wrong, to find a way to be a father to me and a grandfather to our daughter, and that my rejection is a way to control him and not the other way around.

"Honestly, I never thought about it that way. I never thought that by refusing to accept money from my father I control him and make sure he isn't too close to me. It reminded me of something you said about how money and sex are areas that people are most dishonest and hypo-critical about. I mean, my father supported my mother and me financially all those years. I never thanked him, even though I knew he wasn't wealthy and therefore had to sacrifice. I didn't thank him for the gifts he sent me, not for the summer camps or the college tuition he paid, not for the big trip I took after I graduated. I didn't want to feel that I needed him or to give him that power over us. I felt that it was his responsibility to pay. The truth is that sometimes I felt that I was doing him a favor by letting him give me money, as if it was something I gave him and not the other way around. Now I want to do it differently, to be able to give him something by accepting his money and to feel appreciative for what he gives me. What do you think, Galit, does it make sense to accept his offer?"

I think about the betrayal of her mother, wondering if Alice is aware that it was her conflict of loyalty that prevented her from thanking her father for anything he gave her. If she let herself know that she missed her father, that she needed him, she might be breaking her mother's heart again. She had to make herself forget about her father. Now she is asking for my permission to let him in and to forgive him.

Alice's emotional growth is as speedy as her speech. I witness her picture beginning to be filled in with nuances, as she adds more colors to what used to be a black-and-white split view of her parents. She can now let herself see both of them as humans who struggle to be happy. She acknowledges the different ways they each used her in their divorce, treating her as a valuable asset that they were not willing to share.

I recognize the tender love Alice has for them and her pain at not being able to start over, to heal her parents, bring them together, and live her childhood again.

It is time to mourn, to treat her own wounds, and to liberate her future.

"I want to let myself be my father's daughter," Alice says.

I know what she means. She doesn't want to end up envying her daughter for having the father she never had. She doesn't want to repeat her history.

Unlike the fantasy that one's life starts or ends when a baby is born, life, and so, too, the process of examining it, is ongoing. There are many layers that Alice will have to peel away and explore as she gets closer to her emotional truth. She will relive her childhood with every stage of her daughter's life. She will need to be angry at her parents and forgive them again. She will try to do her best, exactly the way her mother did, and will realize that her best isn't always good enough. She will make mistakes and question herself, find herself overcorrecting for her parents' faults as well as repeating them. She will feel gratitude for what they gave her, knowing that they were limited in their ability to know themselves and to work through their traumatic pasts, and that she had to do some of that work for them.

Alice will never forget the painful yet fortunate journey of bringing Zoe to life. She and I will keep searching for her truths; she will try to own her past and question what she doesn't yet know about herself and about life.

In the end, we come to realize that it is the unexamined lives of others that we ourselves end up living.

A Door Opens

THE ABILITY TO love, to invest in life, to create and fulfill our dreams, is in ongoing dialogue with our capacity to search for emotional truths, to tolerate pain, and to mourn.

While our journeys to healing vary, each starts with the decision to search, to open the door, and, rather than turn away from the hurt of the past, to walk toward it. We choose to unpack our emotional inheritance, to be active agents in transforming our fate into destiny.

The secrets of others become our own enigmas, and our secrets will inevitably find shelter and hide in the minds of others. The more concealed these secrets are, the more we become strangers to ourselves, held in captivity, afraid of the freedom to know and be known. The ghosts of the past are alive in our unconscious. To some degree, we are all gatekeepers of the unspeakable.

The scars of our inherited trauma take their own unique shape. Our awareness, like detective work, follows the traces those ghosts leave in our minds. This awareness slowly sheds light on the ways the past affects and controls our present being. In ways that often feel mysterious, emotional material left unprocessed tends to appear and reappear in our lives. The unexamined life repeats itself and reverberates through the generations. The untold stories clamor for reenactment — they insist on being told. That which cannot be consciously identified forces itself into our reality and repeats itself. It is those now-seen patterns that we search for and unpack.

Again and again, the human unconscious brings us to the original site of where things went wrong with the wish to do it all over again, repair the damage, and heal those who were hurt and wounded. We identify with previous generations — with those who have been injured, who have been humiliated, and who have died. In our fantasy, their cure is also our own. We plead for liberation from our bonds to the painful past and from the guilt of living and having a better life than the people who came before us.

However, that unconscious wish to heal our ancestors often prevents us from mourning everything we cannot repair, save, or start again: our own childhoods, our parents' wounds, and our grandparents' trauma. It is the process of mourning and working through the pain that our parents couldn't endure that paves the way to breaking the identification with those who suffered. Mourning differentiates the past from the present and separates those who died from those who stayed alive. We mourn what was out of our control, and therefore we mourn our lack of omnipotence, the fact that in reality we are not as powerful as we are in our fantasies. That emotional truth — our mortality, inherent vulnerability, and human limitations — leaves us humble and allows us to explore who we really are, to embrace future possibilities, and to raise the next generation with dignity.

Ending the intergenerational cycle of suffering is expressed in the quote from Jeremiah with which I open this book — the wish that in the future "people will no longer say, 'The parents have eaten sour grapes, and the children's teeth are set on edge'" (31:29). This is a prayer that children won't have to carry the consequences of their parents' lives, and the wish that our emotional inheritance can be worked through and altered.

For years, we were used to accepting genetic heritage as fate. Biologists believed that environmental factors had little, if any, effect on DNA and that therefore psychological growth was separated from our genetic legacy. These days, the field of epigenetics gives us another framework for understanding how nature and nurture intermingle and how we respond to the environment on a molecular level. It emphasizes that genes have a "memory" that can be passed down from one generation to the next.

The implications for this new research are bidirectional: we realize that trauma can be transmitted to the next generation but also that psychological work can alter and modify the biological effects of trauma. Stephen Stahl, professor of psychiatry at the University of California, San Diego, argues that psychotherapy can be conceptualized as an "epigenetic drug" since it changes the circuitry of the brain in a manner similar to or complementary to drugs. Our hope lies in the understanding that our emotional work has a profound effect on who we, our children, and our grandchildren will become. Trauma is transmitted through our minds and through our bodies, but so are resilience and healing.

The next generations carry not only the despair of the past, but also hope, because their mere existence is evidence that their family survived and that a future is possible. Reliving our ancestors' pain allows us to reference the traumatic past as a way to imagine a possible future, a trajectory from chaos to order, from helplessness to agency, and from destruction to re-creation. In that sense, our work is a way to process and recall past liberation, and also look forward to future redemption.

A DOOR OPENS

When we can learn to identify the emotional inheritance that lives within us, things start to make sense and our lives begin to change. Slowly, a door opens, a gateway between present life and past trauma. On our way to healing, that which seemed impossible now becomes tangible, the pain diminishes, and a new path appears — to love.

Acknowledgments

THIS BOOK IS dedicated to the memory of Lewis Aron, whose devoted love, incredible wisdom, and constant support are always with me.

My enormous gratitude goes to my patients, those whom I've written about and those whose stories are carried in my heart. Thank you for teaching me so much about the human mind and about myself. The patients whose stories are in this book helped me to alter the details and disguise their identities. Thank you for inviting me to join your journeys, for trusting me to write your stories, and for reading those chapters with so much insight and generosity.

I'm blessed to be part of the incredible community of the New York University Postdoctoral Program in Psychotherapy and Psychoanalysis. I'm especially grateful to my dear colleagues, students, and friends who have read and commented on early versions of these chapters: Dr. Jessica Benjamin, Dr. Carina Grossmark, Dr. Jonathon Slavin, Karen Tocatly, Dr. Velleda Ceccoli, Nina Smilow, Dr. Yael Kapeliuk, Colette Linnihan, Dr. Noga Ariel-Galor, Dr. Lauren Levine, Kristin Long, Avital Woods, Dr. Merav Roth, Dr. Robert Grossmark, Dr. Yifat Eitan-Persico, Ivri Lider, Orly Vilnai, Anat Binur, Limor Laniado-Tiroche, Jamie Ryerson, and Amy Gross. To Dr. Roberto Colangeli for sharing with me his work on epigenetics and psychoanalysis. To Dr. Judith Alpert for her help on the chapter on sexual abuse. To Dr. Beatrice Beebe for her inspiration and edits of the chapter on babies. To Ezra Miller for their helpful guidance on gender binary.

A special thank you to Dr. Melanie Suchet for her generous ongoing love and support.

To Dr. Steve Kuchuck for his invaluable contribution to this book and for years of friendship and creative collaboration. I couldn't do it without your talent, wit, and loyalty.

About ten years ago, aiming to investigate psychoanalytic "ghosts," I joined a group of psychoanalysts in New York City who were analyzing the many ways in which ghosts appear in our practices. I would like to thank Adriene Harris and the group: Margery Kalb, Susan Klebanoff, Heather Ferguson, Michael Feldman, and Arthur Fox.

ACKNOWLEDGMENTS

Many thanks to Emma Sweeney, who held my hand and believed in this book before it was born. Thank you for your insightful advice and deep care. Thanks also to Margaret Sutherland Brown at Folio. A special thank-you to my wonderful agent Gail Ross.

I'm deeply grateful to Sally Arteseros for her remarkably keen eye and endless dedication. I'm so lucky to have you be part of this creation.

I feel incredibly fortunate to have Tracy Behar as my editor and publisher. Thank you for your brilliant work and for believing in this book and in me. Thank you for your close reading, deep attention, thoughtful guidance, and unique ability to respond not only to the words on the page, but also to the words that need to be there.

To the extraordinary group at Little, Brown Spark: Ian Straus, Betsy Uhrig, Laura Mamelok, Lucy Kim, Jessica Chun, Juliana Horbachevsky, and Lauren Ortiz. To Sally-Anne McCartin of McCartin Daniels PR.

To Bob Miller, who is my rock and my sanctuary. Thank you for joining me on a constant search for emotional truths, for always being there to catch me, for reading every word I write with curiosity and breathtaking intelligence. Thank you for sharing with me your gifted mind and soul and for loving me the way you do.

To my family, whom I love endlessly: my parents, Shoshi and Yaakov Atlas, who taught me everything I know about

ACKNOWLEDGMENTS

love and dedication. To my sister, Keren Atlas-Dror, who was my first real witness and supporter. To Ashi Atlas, Anat Rose-Atlas, Tamir Koch, Mika and Itamar Dror. To my beloved stepchildren, Benjamin, Raphi, and Kirya Ades-Aron, for being with me through so much and for the family that we are for each other forever.

Above all, I want to thank my children, Emma, Yali, and Mia Koch. You inspire me, surprise me, move me, and teach me something new every day. Thank you for being the people you are and the best family one could ever dream of.

About the Author

Galit Atlas, PhD, is a psychoanalyst and clinical supervisor in private practice in New York City. She is a faculty member of the New York University Postdoctoral Program in Psychotherapy and Psychoanalysis. She is a faculty member of the National Training Program and the Four Year Adult Training Program of the National Institute for the Psychotherapies in New York City. Dr. Atlas has published three books for clinicians and numerous articles and book chapters that focus primarily on gender and sexuality. Her *New York Times* publication "A Tale of Two Twins" was the winner of a 2016 Gradiva Award. A leader in the field of relational psychoanalysis, Dr. Atlas is a recipient of the André François Research Award and the NADTA Research Award. She teaches and lectures throughout the United States and internationally.